A UNION SOLDIER
IN THE LAND OF THE
VANQUISHED

By the Same Author

JOHN LETCHER OF VIRGINIA:
THE STORY OF VIRGINIA'S CIVIL WAR GOVERNOR
(Southern Historical Publications No. 11)

Southern Historical Publications No. 13

A UNION SOLDIER IN THE LAND OF THE VANQUISHED

The Diary of Sergeant Mathew Woodruff, June - December,

1865

Edited and Annotated by

F. N. BONEY

UNIVERSITY OF ALABAMA PRESS

Table of Contents

PREFACE
vi

THE DIARY OF SERGEANT MATHEW WOODRUFF
JUNE–DECEMBER, 1865
3

SELECT BIBLIOGRAPHY
91

INDEX
97

Preface

THE HEART OF THIS VOLUME IS THE VERBATIM DIARY OF A UNION
soldier stationed in the deep South immediately after the Civil
War. Wherever possible people, places, and events have been
identified in a series of footnotes, but the actual language of the
diary has been almost entirely unaltered. Misspellings, gram-
matical errors, and other obvious literary flaws have been
tolerated in order to preserve the original flavor of the docu-
ment. Only where absolutely necessary for clarity have editorial
corrections been introduced into the natural flow of the narra-
tive. Thus, Sergeant Mathew Woodruff is allowed to have his
say, while the editor stays where he belongs, out of sight and out
of mind.

This book would have been impossible without the coopera-
tion of many persons and institutions. Basic to the whole project
was the permission of the Henry E. Huntington Library to use

and publish the diary. Then research assistance came from all over the country, especially the Ohio Historical Society, the State Historical Society of Missouri, the University of Missouri Library, the Adjutant General's Office of the State of Missouri, the University of Mississippi Library, the University of Alabama Library, the Louisiana State University Library, and the National Archives. Professor Herbert Boschung of the Alabama Marine Resources Laboratory, Professor Harry J. Bennett of Louisiana State University, Professor Leslie Anders of Central Missouri State College, and Professor Robert M. Sutton of the University of Illinois rendered valuable assistance, and, as always, my wife patiently proofread the entire manuscript. Finally, generous support by Washington State University and the University of Georgia allowed this project to be completed without undue delay.

Athens, Georgia   F. N. BONEY

A UNION SOLDIER
IN THE LAND OF THE
VANQUISHED

The Diary of Sergeant Mathew Woodruff,
June - December, 1865

MATHEW WOODRUFF, A LEAN, DARK-HAIRED FARM BOY, GREW UP near Watertown in Washington County, Ohio. Intelligent but not well educated, ambitious but unskilled, puritanical but quick to backslide, provincial but restless, this rather typical young American joined the endless westward folk movement before his eighteenth year. Drifting almost due west, he finally settled near the little town of St. Francisville, in northeastern Missouri, and began to ply the only trade he knew, farming.

Suddenly the rhythm of life on the land was disrupted by the distant roar of cannons in Charleston harbor. Years of sectional controversy, which Mathew Woodruff had hardly noticed, finally tore the nation violently asunder and altered the course of every American's life. The South quickly became the Confederacy; the North remained the Union. Along the new, fluid border people and whole states watched in dismay and confusion. Nowhere was the coming holocaust more truly and

3

tragically a *civil* war than in the border slave state of Missouri. Amidst waves of violence Missouri wavered but finally held with the Union, though a sizeable minority of the state's young men joined the rebel legions.

Woodruff and thousands and thousands of other adventurous young men, eager for a change and a challenge, rushed to don Union blue or rebel grey. Unlike so many Missourians, Woodruff had no doubt where his allegiance lay. His roots were deep in Northern soil, and his new home in Clark County, Missouri, as far north as Indianapolis or Philadelphia and just across the Des Moines River from Illinois, was not oriented toward the South. Woodruff did not really know the South. He had little respect for its traditions, less fear of its power, and no liking for slavery or, one surmises, for the Negro.[1]

Without hesitation he chose the Union, joining the 2nd Northeast Missouri Infantry Regiment on June 15, 1861. Tall and muscular, hardened by outdoor labor, he was physically ready for army life, for endless marches and long bivouacs in every kind of weather and, inevitably, bloody clashes with the lean, tough farmers of the South—men and boys who often differed from him in little more than the color of their uniforms.

The war began soon enough for Woodruff and his comrades. Training and maneuvers occupied these raw young troopers for the rest of the year. Then, early in 1862, Woodruff's unit

[1] Service Record of Mathew Woodruff, Compiled Service Records of Volunteer Union Soldiers Who Served in Organizations from the State of Missouri, National Archives, Washington, D.C.; Service Record of Mathew Woodruff, Adjutant General's Office, State of Missouri, Jefferson City, Missouri; J. G. Randall and David Donald, *The Civil War and Reconstruction* (Boston: D. C. Heath and Company, 1961), pp. 234–236; Walter Williams. *The State of Missouri: An Autobiography* (Columbia, Missouri: Press of E. W. Stephens, 1904), pp. 360–361; The Diary of Sergeant Mathew Woodruff, June–December, 1865, *passim*.

was merged with another similar local outfit into the 21st Missouri Volunteer Infantry Regiment, and in March the new regiment, though barely organized, marched proudly to Pittsburg Landing in southern Tennessee, as Union forces knifed into the Confederacy along the Tennessee River. Suddenly it was engulfed in the savage battle of Shiloh, one of the bloodiest engagements of the whole war. Game but green, the citizen-soldiers of the 21st Missouri were no more ready for combat than were the grey hordes that surged toward them out of the misty dawn. Part of General Benjamin W. Prentiss' new Sixth Division, Army of the Tennessee, the 21st Missouri was the first regiment to fire into the attacking rebels and the first to be bloodied in return. Despite heavy losses, the 21st fought gallantly as the Sixth Division disintegrated in the whirl of battle. After two days of indecisive slaughter, the battered Confederate forces retreated toward Corinth, Mississippi, leaving the equally battered Union troops in possession of the field. Woodruff and his surviving comrades, most of them boys-turned-men overnight, were fast becoming veterans. They were certainly not iron-disciplined professionals, for these hardy, freedom-loving young Americans had little or no interest in military careers. Nevertheless, they were or were fast becoming tough, proficient fighting men who would crush the rebellion or die trying.

The victorious Union army, including the 21st Missouri, waited for reinforcements and then slowly moved against the rebel forces at Corinth. Thus, after a bloody baptism of fire at Shiloh, the 21st Missouri marched on into three more years of wartime service. The battles of Iuka and Corinth and other campaigns in Mississippi followed before the end of the year. Then came a year of garrison duty in Tennessee and Kentucky, followed by further grueling campaigns like the ill-fated Red River Expedition, savage battles like Pleasant Hill and Tupelo, and many additional skirmishes all over the western theater of

operations. Woodruff survived the relentless attrition of combat, learning the art of war on the firing line, and by the summer of 1864 he was first sergeant of Company G. Many of his
closest friends had fallen, and he too had paid a price. Twice
he was hospitalized with debilitating diseases, the invisible en-
emies that decimated every army in the field.

Yet despite every hardship, this weary, 21-year-old veteran
not only served loyally but, along with the majority of his regiment, re-enlisted when his three-year term of service expired.
His elite unit, now the 21st Missouri Veteran Volunteer Infantry Regiment, joined more than 135,000 other irreplaceable
veterans who were willing and able to fight on to final victory.
These experienced troopers, the equal of any fighting men on
earth, were still not professional soldiers, careerists with a
"home in the army"; fundamentally they remained what they
had always been, citizen-soldiers, eager to go home but even
more eager to destroy the weakening armies of the Confederacy.

One of these rebel armies, under General John B. Hood, had
invaded Tennessee; and late in 1864, three divisions of the
Army of the Tennessee, including the 21st Missouri, were
rushed east to help administer a crushing blow to the Confederacy in the bloody battle of Nashville. As usual, Woodruff's regiment performed well, both in the battle and in the
swift pursuit of the disintegrating rebel army fleeing into Mississippi.

Everywhere the Southern armies were collapsing, and with
the dawn of the new year of 1865 the war to preserve the Union
was practically won. For Sergeant Woodruff and his comrades
only one minor campaign remained, the capture of the city of
Mobile. Since Mobile Bay was already controlled by the United
States Navy, the city itself had little military value; nevertheless, 45,000 Union troops, including the 21st Missouri, were diverted to capture it. Outnumbering the defenders better than

four to one, the Union forces closed in rapidly. By April, only
Spanish Fort and Fort Blakely on the eastern approaches to
the city effectively blocked their way. Spanish Fort fell on the
evening of April 8, and on the day following, Palm Sunday—
the day General Lee surrendered in Virginia—the 21st Missouri
and other regiments totaling 16,000 men massed to assault Fort
Blakely. Woodruff and his comrades had one last combat assign-
ment, one last headlong charge, before final victory. The signal
to attack was given, and the 21st Missouri surged forward, in
the thick of the fray as usual. Sergeant Woodruff led Company
G straight toward the flashing rebel defenses—and pitched to
the ground with a bullet in his thigh. Many of his comrades
fell too, but the blue waves quickly swept over the rebel fortifications, and the war was over for the 21st Missouri.[2]

Wounded, not seriously but painfully, Woodruff remained
in an army hospital for a little over a month and then went
home to Missouri on furlough. The following weeks were a
pleasant interlude for the 22-year-old veteran. He relaxed in
a nonmilitary manner, visited old friends, and shyly courted a
local belle, Carrie, whom he had long admired. Then it was
time to return to duty, peacetime duty for the first time in his
army career.

Late in June, Sergeant Woodruff prepared to return to his

2 Service Record of Woodruff, National Archives; Diary of Woodruff,
passim; Regimental Book of the 21st Missouri Infantry, Records of the
Adjutant General's Office, National Archives, Washington, D. C., *passim*;
Randall and Donald, *Civil War and Reconstruction*, pp. 205–207, 409, 453,
523; Stanley F. Horn, *The Decisive Battle of Nashville* (Baton Rouge:
Louisiana State University Press, 1956), *passim*; Bruce Catton, *This Hallowed Ground: The Story of the Union Side of the Civil War* (Garden City,
New York: Doubleday & Company, 1956), pp. 109–119, 313, 317–319, 366–
369; *Battles and Leaders of the Civil War* (New York: The Century Company, 1884), IV, 410–412, 440–74; Walter L. Fleming, *Civil War and Reconstruction in Alabama* (Cleveland, Ohio: The Arthur H. Clark Company,
1911), pp. 70–71.

company, which had been temporarily detached from the rest of the regiment and transferred to Pascagoula, an isolated town on the Gulf coast of Mississippi. The war was won, but the peace was in doubt. Somehow the Union had to be permanently restored. Somehow the conquered Southern states, whatever their legal status, had to be reformed, reconstructed within the victorious Union. Somehow the sullen white and confused black peoples of the former Confederacy had to be made as "American" as the people of the North. Somehow four years of bitterness and chaos had to evolve rapidly into an era of harmony and happiness. Such a broad, effective reconstruction proved to be impossible, for the victors could never really agree on either strategy or objectives, but even limited reform was not likely unless a large, well-disciplined army of occupation was maintained in the South for years.

Like most Americans, however, Sergeant Woodruff believed that military victory had settled everything. He had served faithfully throughout the war, and now his main desire was to return to civilian life. He had no sympathy whatsoever for the bewildered freedmen; and, although he disliked and distrusted former rebels, he was unwilling to remain in the ranks with the regulars long enough to insure the permanency of the Union victory. This desire for rapid demobilization was overwhelming among the victors, soldiers and civilians, and the ranks of the Union army thinned almost as rapidly in victory as the ranks of the Confederate army had thinned in defeat. As the Union army faded, so faded any real chance of permanent reform in the stubbornly conservative South.[3]

But Sergeant Woodruff was not at all concerned with the

[3] Service Record of Woodruff, National Archives; Diary of Woodruff, *passim;* John Hope Franklin, *Reconstruction: After the Civil War* (Chicago: University of Chicago Press, 1961), pp. 35–37 and *passim;* Kenneth M. Stampp, *The Era of Reconstruction: 1865–1877* (New York: Alfred A. Knopf, 1966), *passim.*

weightier aspects of peace and reunion on that day late in June
when he left his sweetheart—almost his fiancee—and began his
journey from northeastern Missouri back to his company in the
deep South. While traveling he began to keep an informal
diary, a hastily written odyssey of his life in the peacetime army
of occupation, an unsophisticated soldier's view of life in the
land of the vanquished.

[*N. B. Words underlined by Sergeant Woodruff are printed in
italic type throughout.*]

29th June [1865]

Traveled by Rail Keokuk to Decatur Ills. stoped over night,
saw for the first time in my life a squad of wild Indians Dressed
in their native garb, going to Jacksonville to show.[4]

30th June

by Rail to Cairo, Ills. put up at Soldiers Rest.[5]

1st July

Embarked on Bd. Stmr, Ida Handy for New Orleans, departed
6 oclock P.M.[6]

[4] Woodruff traveled to Carthage, Illinois, on the Milwaukee & Western
Railroad, then southeast to Clayton via a newly constructed stretch of
track, then on to Meredosia on the Quincy and Toledo line, and finally
due east on the Great Western Railroad through Jacksonville and Springfield to Decatur in central Illinois.

[5] This stretch was covered by the Illinois Central Railroad, a vital transportation artery during the war.

[6] Built in Jeffersonville, Indiana in 1864, this 684-ton paddle-wheeler
plied the Mississippi River as a Union transport in the last months of the
war. She was lost in 1866.

2 July

passed Memphis Tenn. in the evening, did not get to see my old Friends.

3rd July

passed Hellena Ark. 10 oclock A.M.

4th July

Arrived at Vicksburgh Miss. this A.M. 10 oclock. Expected to see great honors displayed, but was disappointed. The people seem to have forgoten the day we celebrate & mooreover they do not realize the fact that 2 years ago this verry day 4 hundred Black Guns looked over the summits of the surrounding hills & threatened their destruction. All seemed to be lost in revelry, such is the effects of war with a civalized Nation. The war is over, but I am sorry to say the people does not do honor to the fallen Braves, or the suffering communities of our Nation.[7]

July 5th

passed Port Hudson and Batonrouge La.[8]

[7] After a relentless siege of over six weeks, Vicksburg and 30,000 Confederate troops surrendered to General U. S. Grant on July 4, 1863. This was a disastrous day for the city and for the entire Confederacy, hardly a day for rejoicing. Not until 1945 did the citizens of Vicksburg once again join their fellow Americans in celebrating national Independence Day.

[8] Port Hudson, the Confederacy's last bastion on the Mississippi River after the fall of Vicksburg, underwent a similar six-week siege by General Nathaniel P. Banks. The capitulation of its 6,000 defenders on July 9, 1863, isolated the Confederate West and prompted President Lincoln to write: "The Father of Waters again goes unvexed to the sea." General Banks had taken Baton Rouge four months earlier.

6th July

arrived at New Orleans in the Morning about 6 oclock. de-
posited our Luggage at Texas House, Cor[ner] Julia and New
Levee St. went to French Market and took Breakfast, and then
to Q. M. Office for Transportation.[9] learned Steamer would
not go out till 6 P.M. so we're off for a stroll through the Citty.
rambled on foot till all are tiredout, find nothing to brighten
my lowly spirit, or relieve my mind of the weighty Burden that
is continualy pulling me down. The pomp & pride of southern
chivalry has no Charms for me. get Bd. of St. Carrs & ride down
to Bks. Hosp[ita]l near the old Btl. ground where Jackson
whaled the Britons on 8th of Jany. 1815. here Packenham was
Killed, shiped in Bbl. of rum on Bd. vessel for England, with
some of the soldiery who drank up the Rum, left old Pack. out
in the dry & had a good time etc.[10] Saw two of my old Co. here
looking well, said they had a good thing of it, & was going to
Keep it. I couldent see it. returned to the city, thence by 4 P.M.

[9] The corner of Julia and New Levee Streets was only two blocks from
the docks where General Benjamin F. ("Beast") Butler and the first Federal
occupation troops landed in the spring of 1862. This area contained many
boarding houses. The French Market was a dozen and a half blocks downstream, just past Jackson Square. It was one of the oldest institutions in
the city and one of the main attractions of the French Quarter, or Vieux
Carré.

[10] The "Bks. Hospl." was part of the barracks complex constructed during the administration of President Andrew Jackson as both a fort and a
garrison area. The main buildings were sturdy, thick-walled, brick structures. The Confederates used these facilities until the fall of New Orleans
when they reverted to Federal control. They continued to house American
troops well into the twentieth century. Sgt. Woodruff could conveniently
reach the barracks via the city's street car system. This system was composed
of single coaches pulled by horses along fixed tracks. A short distance
downstream from the barracks was the famous battlefield where Major
General Sir Edward Pakenham fell. His body was preserved in a barrel of
rum and shipped back to London, but Woodruff's additional description
of the ghoulish consumption of the rum seems to be pure American legend.

Train for lake shore.[11] Embarked on Lake Steamer Allice Vivian for Mobile Ala.[12] All clear of Obstructions at sunset & steaming for Blue Water. I make my Bed at dusk on some Matrasses that are stained with Blood [.] perhaps some of my comrades have yielded up their spirit to god from off this verry Matress on which I sit, or if the Foe it maters not, all are the same after death if they die in the Faith of Jesus. After my short Prayer for absent Loved ones I fall asleep with a strong Breeze blowing full in my face & awake at the Dawn of day the 7th feeling quite refreshed. Now dear one I must leave you for a little while Farewell. We're out on the ocean sailing to a home Beyond The Tide.

7th July

Landed at Ship Island 7 A.M. left some provision for the garrison, stuck on a Bar at Fort Powell. After a little Exertion the old ship dislocated herself & we went on our way rejoicing.

11 The most likely route to an embarkation point was the Pontchartrain Railroad, which ran in a straight line almost due north from the river along Elysian Fields Avenue to Lake Pontchartrain, a distance of only four and a half miles. Built in 1831, it was one of the nation's earliest railroads, and its lakeside terminus, Milneburg, was a vital shipping point for both the Confederate and later the Federal army. This pioneer line was absorbed by the Louisville & Nashville Railroad in 1880 and continued to operate until 1932. Three other rail lines also reached the nearby lakes. The Carrollton Railroad ran a few miles upstream to the Jefferson & Lake Pontchartrain Railroad, which continued on to the lake. The Mexican Gulf Railroad ran downstream and finally ended on the south shore of Lake Borgne, a distance of 27 miles. The New Orleans, Jackson, & Great Northern Railroad—later part of the Illinois Central system—brushed the western shore of Lake Pontchartrain on its way toward Mississippi.

12 The *Alice Vivian*, built in 1856 and displacing 376 tons, regularly made the packet run between Memphis and New Orleans before the war. During the war she served as a rebel blockade runner until captured by the U.S.S. *De Soto* in August, 1863 while carrying cotton toward Havana. The battered old sidewheeler was finally scrapped in 1867.

One unused to these Waters would suppose as they look round, twas verry deep. I find tis not the case in many Instances. touched at Forts Gains and Morgan.[13]

8th July

Arrived at Mobile 10 A.M. hapily. I met 3 of my old Co. here on business who was acquainted with the Beats, so I was soon in the right channel, & in 2 hours was ready to reship for Pascagoula. In the Evening went on Bd. Steam ship Laura.[14]

9th July.

Steamed out from the Pier, 7 A.M. After many delays arrived at my destination 10 A.M. of the 10th July.

[13] Thirty miles south of Biloxi, Ship Island lay astride the direct water route between New Orleans and Mobile. It was captured by Union forces in September, 1861 before Confederate fortifications were complete. It was used as a prisoner of war camp, and it was also the staging area for Flag Officer David G. Farragut's successful attack on New Orleans. A Federal garrison remained on Ship Island until 1875. Forts Powell, Morgan, and Gaines were the guardians of the entrance of Mobile Bay. On August 5, 1864 Admiral Farragut's fleet fought its way into the Bay, but not without receiving a mauling from the guns of Fort Morgan, a pentagonal brick fortress, underwater mines, and a small rebel fleet led by the ram *Tennessee*. Fort Gaines, on the eastern tip of Dauphin Island, was too far from the main channel to be a serious threat, and Fort Powell a few miles upstream was incomplete and easily captured before the end of the day. Fort Gaines, under heavy attack from land and sea, surrendered unconditionally two days later. Mighty Fort Morgan held out stubbornly. Union land and sea forces pounded the rebels relentlessly, and finally the 600-man garrison surrendered on August 23. Although the city of Mobile did not full until the last days of the war, it was henceforth closed to ocean traffic, and only Charleston and Wilmington remained as operative seaports of the Confederacy.

[14] At least eight *Lauras*, Union, Confederate, and British, were active during the Civil War. Woodruff's vessel was probably the Union transport *Laura*, which served in the Gulf campaigns. It was Major General Gordon Granger's headquarters during the battle of Mobile Bay.

Tuesday 11 [July]

Resumed the dutys involving on me as 1st Sergt. of the Company today. found things in a worse condition & the Co. farther behind with Business than when I left it 3 months ago after 14 months of active Field Service & weary campaigning, just 3 months farther in shade. All the men are in good health, glad to see me return. rec'd. a hearty welcome from all.

Wednesday, July 12, 1865

I am well pleased with the Location here. have a fine large Building for quarters. is situated close to the Beach. We always get a sea Breeze when there is one. most a delightful place, can sit on the Balcony an look as far as the eye can reach. have a magnificent view of Round Island & Horn Island in the distance.[15]

Thursday 13 [July]

busied myself at the Desk till Evening, went Bathing in the salt water. bathing I find is verry fashionable pleasure here, freely indulged in by Both sex and all grades and classes. furthermore it is verry essential to good health. Invalids comes from far & near to bathe.

[15] Sleepy Pascagoula had been a popular summer resort area before the war, and a three-story hotel designed to house a thousand guests was built overlooking the sea. This was an ideal barracks for the Federal garrison. See entries for August 6 and September 11. Round Island lay five miles due south of Pascagoula Bay, and long, narrow Horn Island, the larger of the two, was five miles farther out in the Gulf.

Friday 14

The boys take me round and Introduce to their Female acquaintances. mostly creoles, as they call them, but on a close
definition of the word creole, I find those substitutes, are mostly
Mongrells, Negroes, Mulattoes and so on. I found nothing half
so Beautiful, as represented.

Saturday, July 15, 1865

Capt. and I went Fishing, caught some fine Speckled Trout of
which these waters bountifully yield. There is a fish here called
the Redfish, that is nearly equal to the Trout, but grow mutch
larger, are plenty but hard to catch. seem to run in schools &
are verry wild.[16]

Sunday 16

was accepted as a member of Head Quarter Mess, consisting of
the Captain, 2nd Lieut. Meehan, Telegraph Operator, myself
& Pitts a German who is chief cook and cater of the Mess.[17] I
do not have to cook any now, a thing I always dreaded. if I
cant Marry a good cook when I get out of the army, I'll board
by the week.

[16] The redfish, *Sciaenops ocellata,* is still a common fish in the area. It is
also referred to as the red drum and the channel bass. The trout mentioned
is technically not a trout at all but another sciaenid, *Cynoscion arenarius.*
[17] The company commander was Captain Edward K. Blackburn. A veteran
of Shiloh, Nashville, and other bloody battles, he was promoted from first
lieutenant on January 5, 1863. Woodruff mentions him frequently in the
rest of the diary. The licutenant is unidentifiable, and the cook is probably
Private Peter Pitts. (See entries for October 12 and 22.)

Monday 17

Received an Invitation to a cotillion Party at Mr. Conroys on Evening of 19th in the Evening.[18] J.W.B. invited me & Mr. Roseberry to walk up to Mr Cs. & take part in shotish as he had Engaged the Co. of some young Ladys for the occasion.[19] No Ladys appeared. I give it up for a nice sell, for which these people are noted I discover. what would *cousin Lide* say to this.

Tuesday, July 18, 1865

Was quite amused at the oposition between the boys, all so anctious to procure the best looking Partner. had to begin in season, as the only means of Transportation was an old Army Ambulance drawn by an Army Mule, just imagine me & a creole Dame in the Enjoyment of such a luxury, sporting over a fine shell road behind a lame Mule. *Cant see it.*

Wednesday 19

Went to the Party made the acquaintance of a verry beautiful

[18] Fearful of stragglers, deserters, and bushwhackers, Pascagoula, Biloxi, and some other settlements along the Gulf coast actually requested Federal protection early in May, 1865. Thus even the staunchest of rebels might not have been entirely hostile, and southerners who had felt no deep loyalty to the Confederacy would have been even more friendly toward the Yankees. Mr. Conroy and the other residents of Pascagoula mentioned by Woodruff are not identifiable.

[19] "J. W. B." was Sergeant John W. Butcher, one of Woodruff's closest friends who is mentioned frequently in the diary. Drum Major Thomas H. Roseberry was another friend who was soon promoted to sergeant major. The "shotish" (schottische) was a round dance resembling the polka, the "German polka."

young spanish Lady hailing from Verra Cruse Mexico. Miss Cassimere proposed to learn me to talk French & learn me to waltz, if I would learn her to shotish. if I was possessed of any love for a Southern Belle, I would bestow it here. if my Carrie knew what I was saying & doing, she would get jealous of me. I'll be true to my love.

Thursday 20

Evrything passed off agreeable, a splendid time. At day dawn this morning some of the men got jealous of the rest & began to quarrel & then to fight. I. L. rec'd a severe stab in right side of face one in left shoulder, & one in right fore arm. F. A. M. skull fractured, and soon afterwards Lt. R. R. H. threatened with immediate assasination on St. Perpetrator Es-scaped. A. L. H. got the men to quarters and dressed their wounds.[20]

Friday, July 21, 1865

Evry body is on the alert for the perpetrator of yesterdays crimes fail to find him. wound[ed] men seem to rest easy & bid fair for recovery, wounds are not as serious as I at first an-ticipated. called to see the spanish Maiden. Not as Entertain-ing as she was last Evening, think she will not bear acquaintance.

[20] The troopers involved were Private Isaac Longcor, a short, dark veteran of many battles, Corporal Frank A. Massey, who was captured at Shiloh but exchanged in time to see more combat, and Private Alfred L. Harper, another young veteran. Longcor and Harper continued to get into trouble (as future entries in the diary indicate) and finally, on September 5, Harper deserted. The officer threatened was Lieutenant Robert R. Harris, who is mentioned frequently in the diary under less dramatic circumstances.

Saturday 22

Harper was arrested to day and safely lodged in the Guard-
house, wounded men are doing well, begin to meditate their
case, & conclude they are in rather a critical condition. 96th
U. S. C. I. Col. O. Fariola arrives from Mobile on Engineering
Purposes. going to rebuild Piers Levees etc., that have been destroyed during the war.[21]

Sunday 23

Visited my Fair Dame again, spent a few hours with her and

[21] The 96th United States Colored Infantry was originally the Second
Regiment Engineers, Corps de Afrique, which was organized in New Orleans
in August, 1863. This unit built fortifications and other structures in Texas
until the spring of 1864 when it was designated the 96th U.S.C.I. and transferred back to Louisiana. Despite the new name, the unit remained basically
an engineer regiment. It participated in the sieges of Fort Gaines and Fort
Morgan in Mobile Bay, and in the campaign against Mobile itself during the
final months of the war. The 96th was stationed at various points along
the Gulf until January, 1866, when it was demobilized. Like many other
engineer units, its combat losses were light. Lieutenant Colonel Octave
L. F. E. Fariola de Rozzoli, a Belgian born in 1838, joined the Union army
in 1863 as a Captain of Engineers. He was sent to New Orleans and assigned
to the 5th Regiment Infantry, Corps de Afrique, which later became the
77th United States Colored Infantry. Stationed in the New Orleans area,
this unit, too, was primarily engaged in engineering projects. Though
frequently ill, Fariola served capably, and by the end of the war he was a
lieutenant colonel in the 96th U.S.C.I. He was mustered out with this unit.
He failed as a planter in Louisiana in 1866 and moved to Australia. He
farmed for a decade and then spent two more decades as a civil engineer
in that vast land. Then he undertook other engineering projects in Borneo
and Siam where he married and fathered two children. Finally he returned
to America and retired to a veterans' home in Virginia, but he became restless again and moved to Europe. He died in Palermo, Italy, in 1914. While
in the Union army, this adventurous European had shortened his name
to Octave L.F.E. Fariola. Woodruff and other white troopers privately be-
stowed upon him an even shorter nickname, "Frog-eater."

bid her adieu. she leaves the Village this Evening, goes to her Residence 2½ miles west of here on Pascagoula River. have given up the Idea of learning to talk French, she is so far away I can not afford to visit her often.

Monday, July 24, 1865

Went out in the country riding with the captain on the Mules. Eat some whiskey, which by the way is a favorite beverage with the captain on all occasions, and drank some water-mellons. had a verry pleasant ride. on our return went fishing, but meet with poor success.[22]

Tuesday 25

busied myself in writing out charges & specifications against Corpl. F. A. Massey, Privates Isaac Longcor and Alfred L. Harper, all of Co. "G" 21st Mo. I.V.V. the men who performed their gymnastic exorcises in acts of violence on one an others persons, on the morning of the 20th. They drank too many daintys & Eat too much Egg-nog the night before.

Wednesday 26

report circulated that a young Lady of the village was brutally outraged by one of the collored Soldiers of 96th U. S. C. I. donnt think it was verry scrious on her part, nor was it mutch

[22] Again the company commander, Captain Charles K. Blackburn, who remains a close companion of the demon rum throughout the remainder of the diary.

regreted, as she has been heard to say since, that *she* "would not have had it done for a Thousand Dollars" Virtue is of great value in this country or any other, but they cant see it here.

Thursday, July 27, 1865

went fishing with a Snare, made several halls in the sound, found it verry hard work and poor pay. caught a few fish a Small Shark and a number of Stinger Eells, a fish somewhat resembling our water Tortoise in shape, but have no shell on them, but a long tail with a sharp bony stinger. report here says a person stung by them rarely recovers.[23]

Friday 28

passed the greater portion of the day at my desk. in the evening Corpl. Sherrick arrived via Str. from Mobile with Mail, accompanied by my old Bunky, Sergt. Sheeks Now A.O.S. 21st Mo.[24] Enjoyed a sociable chit-chat, & enumerated the Events of our former life since our separation on the Battle-field of Fort Blakely. Also Sergt. Whetstone arrived with 30 days Rations for the Company. Clothing Forrage etc.[25]

[23] The stingray in Gulf waters was and is capable of inflicting a severe wound on the unwary bather, but fatalities were not as numerous as Woodruff thought.

[24] Corporal Joseph Sherrick is mentioned frequently in the diary. Sergeant George W. Sheeks, Acting Orderly Sergeant, was another young veteran of Shiloh, Nashville, and other battles. He was promoted to corporal in the summer of 1864 and was a sergeant by the end of the year.

[25] Sergeant Jasper N. Whetstone was another young combat veteran of the 21st Missouri.

Saturday 29

busied myself Issuing Clothing & Rations, fileing Invoices, & prepareing official Business for the next Mail. in the Evening Whetstone, Clark, Roseberry & I, Visited a neighbors Residence where there was some young Ladys under agreement to Entertain them with music & a shotish.[26] I will say they did not play Butcher on us, we was heartily Entertained. I could not enjoy it. Why, I'll tell you an other time.

Sunday, July 30, 1865

was one of a pleasure party. went sailing on Schooner Onelia to Horn Island, had a good time.[27] I could enjoy it, but all could not. Why, because that damnable Instigater of all Evils, "poison Whiskey" was in the way. As it is on all occasions with Individuals, however I steer my own Bark and it never interferes with me. I can but pitty the weak man.

Monday 31

made out & forwarded Monthly Returns for the past Month & Requisitions for C.C. and G.E. for the Month of August.[28] was necessarily compelled to keep company all night with *whiskey*

[26] The only member of this group not previously identified was Private Abraham J. Clark, a farmer before the war, who had seen just as much combat as his younger comrades.

[27] As mentioned in note 15, Horn Island was only 10 miles out in the Gulf. The *Onelia* and her skipper, Captain Antone, are mentioned again ·in the entry for August 17.

[28] "C. C. and G. E." meant Clothing, Camp and Garrison Equipage.

in a living casket, took lodgeing in the vilage, had the best
bed I have had since I left home. I enjoyed my rest, *suppose my*
"friend" did too. for better Explanations, see future time.[29]

Tuesday, August 1

Sergt. Butcher & escort with Prisoners in charge started via
steamer for Mobile. had an Invitation to eat "Gumbo" for dinner, did not go.[30] too mutch of an evry day occurrence for me
to be a participant. *I cant see it.* To night the boys are out at
Ws again danceing. I am not well [,] cannot take a part, in fact
I do not admire the stile exactly.[31]

Wednesday, August 2, 1865

Carrie, last night I dreamed I was siting beside you reading in
the Bible of Love & Marriage, I broached the subject in regard
to *our* Marriage, you said you dident Know if you could or
could not fulfill your vows, said there were two other men loved
you dearly & wanted to marry you, might pledge your affections
to one of them. I replied as I awoke, when such was the fact,
I wished to leave you in harmony, & my existence to cease for
ever.

[29] No better explanation appears later. "whiskey in a living casket" probably refers to Captain Blackburn, whose bacchanalian adventures frequently shocked Woodruff. However, in Woodruff's view, this description would
have fit many other troopers in his company too.

[30] "Gumbo," a Creole favorite, was a soup thickened with the mucila-
ginous pods of okra.

[31] "W" refers to a Mr. Welch, a friendly resident (see the entry for August
4). In Woodruff's handwriting, the word "stile" (i.e., style) could be "still,"
but this seems unlikely.

Thursday 3

Martin W. Bates and Jacob Glessner Privates released from confinement in Military Prison Mobile Ala. and joined Company for duty.[32] Madam Rumor says we are going to be relieved from this Post. That look of derision, that scowl turned upon me this morning by Mr. B. as he handed me a letter of which he knew the hand writing[.] I smiled as I rec'd. it.

Friday 4

rained biger part of the day, first rain have had for some time, passed the day in reading of "Jobs" Afflictions etc. Slept some, in the Evening went to Mr. Welchs to dance shotish cotillion etc. lost all the confidence in southern Women I ever possessed. by a flank movement on promenade, I got close enough to one to hold her by the tips of her fingers and stand upright.

Saturday, August 5, 1865

Went fishing caught some fine Red fish & some Trout. wrote out Furlough for Sergt. John W. Butcher. late in the evening patroll guard arrested & brough[t] in 5 soldiers of 96th U.S.C.I. who have been disturbing the peace of the Neighborhood for some nights & plundering anything they could appropriate to their benefit. some shots were exchanged, but without Effect.

[32] Private Martin W. Bates enlisted in the first year of the war at 16 and fought in many bloody battles. Constantly in trouble, he finally deserted. (See entry for August 18.) Private Jacob Glessner, older and more mature, also enlisted early and saw much combat. This was not his last confinement (see entry for November 10), and he too finally deserted, on December 11.

Sunday 6

Capt. B. concludes he must go sailing, & so fires on a schooner laying in the sound to attract her attention, but by the way, he is arrested by col. Fariola.[33] A grand parade in the Evening in front of hotel. Some Navy men attempt a parade at the same place, are drunk. are arrested & confined in Negroe guard house.

Monday 7

the Capt. cannot see his arrest & goes sailing to day. The citizens hold an Election in the Village to Elect state representatives, get so drunk our boy[s] have to carry them home & put them to bed. Then I have to arrest the boys and put *them* to bed. *dat makes mootch trouble mid me,* and the whole company. I have not learned who was elected.[34]

Tuesday, August 8, 1865

went out with the capt. in sail Boat to fish. was caught midway

33 Obviously Captain Blackburn again
34 Provisional Governor William L. Sharkey ordered that county elections be held on August 7 to select delegates to a state convention scheduled to assemble at Jackson on August 14. A majority of the elected delegates were old Whigs. Most of these men had opposed secession, but they backed the Confederacy when war came. Within the context of the times, they might well be labeled "moderates," but to Woodruff and his comrades every Confederate, no matter how much he had opposed secession before the war, was a "traitor." The convention formally abolished slavery, declared secession "null and void," and even granted Negroes some civil rights (but it did not grant them any *political* rights) . Again, within the context of the times, the convention could be labeled "moderate," "conservative," or even "reactionary" depending on the viewpoint of the observer. A century later historians with differing perspectives on the matter still argue over the proper terminology and interpretation.

the Sound in a calm so we threw out our hooks for a bite. capt. caught a catfish, I caught a large Shark 3 feet long. had no fresh water, co[n]sequently was verry thirsty. Came a Breeze we steered our Bark for Quarters

Wednesday 9

3 Negroes Deserted last night. col. bids $30. Each for their apprehension. & delivery. co. is all on the alert. Yealey & I mounts a mule Each & go in pursuit strike the trail follow 7½ miles.[35] here we learn some officers are ahead of us. determined not to share in the Game unless we can have all we turn back. Offs. overhall them 15 ms. ahead & are beaten. return & are arrested for their conduct. *A good joke.*

Thursday 10

drew and Issued C.C. & G.E. for month of August. spend remainder of the day in overhauling & classing old Ordnance returns for the capt. That makes mutch trouble mid me again. go out in the Evening for a bath[,] sea is verry ruff, have fine sport riding the waves. forward Tri M. returns.[36]

Friday, August 11, 1865

Spend the day in making out Clothing Schedules & charging the two last Issues on Company Books. verry tiresome to sit at the desk & write all day. too confineing for me to follow for a

[35] Private Alfred Yealey, a farmer from Iowa, did not enlist until January 2, 1864, but he saw much combat before the war ended.

[36] Tri Monthly Returns were only a fraction of the paperwork that constantly plagued Sergeant Woodruff. (See the next entry.)

lively hood. I offtimes wish it could agree with me. I like . . .
it so well.

Saturday 12

went fishing caug[ht] a fine mess of trout. came back & found our
cook minus. went all day without my dinner. came supper time
no cook, I play Kitchen maid and get supper & wash the dishes.
by the way our *Maid* is of the Masculine Gender. is out on a
drunk. is reprimanded by all on his return.

Sunday 13

Company Inspection this morning. spend the rest of the day
in writing at the desk. go out to see the girls in the Evening but
they all have Co. those that have not cannot have mine. Alvis
Bros. return from Hospl. both were wound[ed] at Blakely when
I was but are well now,[37]

Monday, August 14, 1865

was Employed making monthly returns of Q.M. Stores. Some
of the boys get in a weaving way & raise a mess with an Irish
reb. Arrested & mark time 4 hours under Nigger guard. released
under sentence of paying for property destroyed, and doing
4 days extra duty.

Tuesday 15

worked hard all day on Muster-out rolls of a Det of 8 men who

---

37 Privates Hiram J. and Edward H. Alvis were veteran troopers.

were Transfered to Co. from 24st Mo. Infty. Vols. on 1st day of Feb. 1865 at Eastport Miss.[38] finish them in Evening. boys are ready to go to Mobile Via. first Steamer and be mustered out. all overjoyed at the prospect.

Wednesday 16

men in Camp get on a general spree, two of them went in to a private house & because they refuse to sell them whiskey, one of them *Martin W. Bates* Knocks the old man down & chokes him, then strikes the old Lady over the Eye inflicting a ghastly wound. Guard appears & arrests him, turns round & assaults the Guard who Knocks him down & threatens him so hard with his life, that he begs mercifully.

Thursday, August 17, 1865

Make out Muster-out rolls for Drafted man. Capt. Antone— of schooner Onelia for insulting one of our men is arrested & confined in Guard House of 96" U.S.C.I. with some of our men, who seem to think it a great punishment to *mark time* 4 or 6 hours under a Negroe guard. but they dont heed it. for no sooner are they out than they are off in mischief again.

Friday 18

I am verry unwell nearly confined with a cold. however work

38 By February, 1865 the 24th Missouri Infantry Regiment was mustered out of service, with the exception of a few troopers in understrengthened Companies G and H. By special orders these unhappy few were transferred to the 21st Missouri at Eastport, Mississippi on February 1, 1865, and thus they were fated to remain in the ranks for six more months. The 24th Missouri, organized late in 1861, had participated in many battles in the west. It lost a total of 264 men, only 43 to enemy action, the rest to disease.

must go on. make out Tri M. Returns & forward them. *Bates,*
our fighting man, whom I can call nothing Else but a Kansas
ruff (he is from Kansas) Deserted last night. he is a fine looking
young man of 18, but a verry bad character. was court-martialed
last summer, was in prison under sentence again & was released
a week ago by promising to reform. we see how he did it.

Saturday 19

Make out invoice & recpts. for C.C. & G.E. and . . . ordnance
stores to be turned over on the next trip to Mobile. spend the
remainder of the day on Capts old returns & find him in Debt
to Government so far I fear he never will get out. go out with
Torch & spear in Evening fishing for flounders. dident catch a
gol darn clam.

Sunday, August 20, 1865

Company Inspection 8 oclock this morning. 2" Lt. Harris in
charge of 9 men whose time is out start for Mobile to get them
Mustered out. Yealey and I get up the Mules for a ride, go six
or seven Miles in the country and have a fine time. get some
Water Mellons to Eat, and see the fashions.

Monday 21

spent most of the day in makeing out ordnance returns for the
2nd Qr 1865. went out floundering in the evening dident find
a clam, found a nigger with a cast-net fishing for mullets,
turned in with him & by midnight had a fine Mess for all, I
considered them well earned, for I was verry tired.

Tuesday 22

Made out an Estimate of Clothing, Camp and Garrison Equipage for the month of September. had fine sport over a joke got
off on the Editor of the No-Nothing or Country Chronical,
which has just been started in town. The Editor calls himself
Grizly-Bear.[39] The joke if you had him Grizly Bear by the tail,
would you think it advisable to hold fast, or let go. The ladys
see the point, & talk of Pistols, Knives, Blood etc.

Wednesday, August 23, 1865

96" U.S.C.I. are Ordered to march, get all ready evry thing at
the wharf and the Order is countermanded. Corpl. F. A. Massey
and Privates A. L. Harper & Isaac Longcor are released from
confinement & join Company for duty. Capt. & I went fishing
but have no good luck. our boat is lost now & we have not so
good a chance to fish as we have had.

Thursday 24

Wind has been high for several days threatening rain but get
none, verry dry for 2 weeks back. Guard from 11" Wis. Vols.
brings 2 deserters from Mobile belonging to 96" U.S.C.I.[40]
went out at night with torch & spear to catch flounders but get

[39] This probably refers to the Pascagoula *Chronicle-Star*, which was pub-
lished sporadically during this period. Unfortunately, no copies of this
journal for this period are available, and the editor is unidentifiable.

[40] The 11th Wisconsin Volunteer Infantry was a seasoned regiment that
had served under Grant in the Vicksburg campaign. It fought alongside the
21st Missouri at Fort Blakely. In the course of the war it lost 86 men in
combat and another 257 to various diseases.

none. caught 3 larg[e] stinger Ells. had real merry sport but
verry wearisome & poor pay.

Friday 25

Commenced rai[ni]ng in the afternoon & rains all night. Sergt.
Jno. W. Butcher and Pvt. C. McMichael starts for home on 30
day Furlough.[41] I expect there will be a happy meeting on the
part of J.W.B. and Cousin Lide, then the light heart of a
newly weded Bride must so soon be made sad for the absence
of her groom. how rash, what folly Indeed.

Saturday, August 26, 1865

went with Lt. Harris to see a couple of Ladys by name of
Pickett Miss. Maggie and Miss. Allice, and eat scopenons (a
Kind of Grape that grows in the south & are verry delicious.) [42]
in the Evening the Capt. and I called on Mrs. Parker who
favored us with Music on the Pianno, played and sung for us,
Mary of Argile, Love not, Will you go a Sailing etc.[43]

Sunday 27

make out requisition for rations & forrage. C.S. Sergt. and Corpl.

[41] Private Charles McMichael, a tall, blond farmer, served throughout
the war as a combat soldier. He was promoted to first sergeant in 1863, but
he was soon reduced to the ranks, and he remained a private for the rest
of his military career.

[42] The scuppernong is a native American grape of the muscadine class.
This large, yellow-green fruit made an aromatic wine that was popular in
the South but not greatly admired by connoisseurs.

[43] These were popular songs of the day. "Mary of Argile," a Scottish
ballad, was a favorite of Abraham Lincoln. Mrs. Parker is unidentifiable.

James with 4 men proceed to Mobile to draw rations, hear good News, Viz, that Orders have reached Mobile to Muster Out all white Troops in Dept. of Ala.[44] we will come under that Order if they consider us white. I cant really say I think they do of late.

Monday 28

received one months supplies for Co. from Mobile Ala. up nearly all night takeing Care of them. Capt. goes out riding on Mule gets beastly drunk and falls off 3 times ere he gets to Quarters. if we had an artist here we could present some of the most striking Comic pictures, only think of a Fed. Off. thrown from a Mule, who is running off in glee, & Mr. Capt. left sprawling mid dozens of Juvenile Niggers.

Tuesday, August 29, 1865

Capt. lends the Wagon & Mules to the Telegraph Opr. & others to go riding with some Ladys. accordingly all are set at 3 P.M. & get about a mile out of town when along comes Mr. Capt. who is drunk again as usual & has forgot he loaned the team, so he orders a guard after them, brings them back & after some Brandy *slang* unloads them in the street to walk home and orders the team to QRS. *Gentlemanly like.*

Wednesday 30

was up Town last night to a dance, took no part. got up by the

[44] The Commissary of Subsistence Sergeant and Corporal Amos James were responsible for drawing rations. The good news turned out to be premature.

Officers of 96" U.S.C.I. was mutch diverted by the *Stiles* such agony, & so ignorant of dancing, perfectly disgusting. our Musicians played for them all night and did not even get their suppers. *Stoughton Bottle* goes out riding and falls off Mule.[45] *how are you Uncle.* Btl. is too full overbalanced. I shall call him by this name hereafter & tell you who it is some other time if you dont understand it.

Thursday 31

went fishing caught fine mess of Trout. Corpl. and Guard brings home our boat which they discovered secreted in mouth of Pascagoula River. Make out Muster Roll and Co. Musters for pay. Stoughton is placed in arrest by *Frog-Eater* (col. O. Farriola 96" U.S.C.I.) for insulting women, by telling them he would Bayonet them in *abdomen,* best thing he knew of for Traitors. Invited to participate in a pleasure excursion on the Morrow. Cant see it yet.

Friday, September 1, 1865

was mistaken about *Stoughton* being arrested yesterday only reprimanded. The pleasure party started out at dawn. Insisted that I should go. said they was going where there was *Bear* and *Deer* in abundance, and sutch fine fish to be caught. Would not go. was pleased to learn it was a complete sell and to think I was wise enough to stay at home. Officers and their coquetish sports are haveing a Ball on the lower floor tonight.

[45] "Stoughton Bottle" is mentioned frequently (see especially entries for October 6 and 7) , but he is never identified.

Saturday 2

worked hard all day makeing out Muster and Pay Rolls. went
Bathing in the Evening, and then called on Mrs. Parker who
favores us with some of her sweet melodies on Pianno Forte.
it has been fallen weather for 2 or 3 days and I notice at sutch
time my wound is verry painful, so mutch so, I have nearly de-
termined to have the bullet taken out.

Sunday 3

feel unwell thigh is verry sore. Corporal Sherrick goes to Mobile
by Steamer Magnolia for Mail, Magnolia was towing Steamer
Rein Deer that was blown up a few days ago near N.O. takeing
her to Mobile for repairs.[46] Frog-Eater arrests A.L.H. for Ne-
glect of duty and disobedience of orders and confines him under collored guard, also arrests I.L. & confines him to quarters.[47]

[46] Several *Magnolias* were active during the Civil War period. This one
was probably the former Confederate steamer that was captured off Mobile
early in 1862 while trying to dash from New Orleans to Havana with a load
of cotton. The Union warships *Brooklyn* and *South Carolina* caught the
fleeing vessel and frustrated the efforts of her crew to scuttle her. The
Magnolia was soon repaired and operating again under new colors. The
Union already had another *Magnolia,* a river transport that performed
yeoman service throughout the war. There were also several *Reindeers* during this period. The one mentioned was probably *Reindeer 57,* purchased by
the Union navy in the spring of 1864. One of the *Reindeer's* boilers ex-
ploded, killing 3 and wounding 25 of her crew. The *Magnolia* got the badly
damaged vessel to New Orleans on September 5. Eventually, she was repaired and put back into service.

[47] Colonel Fariola punishes Privates Alfred L. Harper and Isaac Longcor,
Company G's tireless troublemakers. Harper deserted the next evening.
(See entries for September 5 and 6.)

Monday, September 4, 1865

has been Blowing for some days & verry hard by spells with
showers. my wound still continues painful. Can scarcely go up
& down stairs. work on muster rolls, Steamer returns but did
not bring our Mail Messenger. getting so impatient I dont
Know how to be contented. tis now over two weeks since I heard
from *Carrie* although I have written twice.

Tuesday 5

my wound is geting better again not so painful can go about
my duty without Inconve[ni]ence. completed Muster and Pay
rolls. A. L. Harper Pvt. Deserted from confinement last night.
Corpl. Sherrick returns with Mail. Nothing from my Carrie
what suspense, am I forsaken, cant believe it. wind increases &
Blows a severe gale for 3 hours with heavy rain. sea is verry
rough.

Wednesday 6

rather a Mysterious letter makes its appearance on the Captains Desk it is written with pencil and the well Known hand
of A. L. Harper, and is addressed to Capt. Blackburn, telling
him that he (H.) is under false chs. & is not going to stay to
see them, that he is going to Desert without a cent to help him,
that he is a ruined Man & asks capt. to write and tell his Mother
he is gone, as he never will. asks to be remembered with respect
by Co. "G"

Thursday, September 7, 1865

wind continues high with Occasional showers. rec'd an Order
to go to Mobile Via first Steamer to purchase rations for *our*
Mess, and transact other Business for Co. do not feel any further inconvenience from my wound. feel some symtoms of that
dreaded camp scourge Known as Diarrhoea. also symtoms of
schurvy begin to appear in Co. Vegetables are scarce here.[48]

Friday 8

Make-Out Tri Monthly Returns for 10" Sept. has to be done
prior to date in order to reach HdQr. in time. I am patiently
waiting arrival of Str. as I am anxious to get to the city thinking
theres Mail there for me. Offs. 96" have a Ball tonight invited
our officers. Qr. Mr. hints there will not be Gents Enoug[h] to
make interesting[,] does not ask me so *I see the point* & conclude not to honor them with my presence. not in verry amiable
mood for danceing at present.

Saturday 9

saw the Ball room verry nicely decorated with Emblems of
Love. Cedar Boughs, & then a fine large U.S. flag stitched over
head the full length of the hall. and some of the Ladys that

[48] Diarrhea and dysentery, two diseases so closely related that it is difficult to distinguish one from the other, caused more death und sickness than
anything else during the war. Scurvy was also a real but less deadly menace.
Both the Union and Confederate armies were ravaged by these and other
diseases, such as typhoid fever, pneumonia, malaria, smallpox, measles, scar-
let fever, erysipelas, syphilis, and gonorrhea, and the Confederate surrender
did not end the Union army's fight against disease.

danced on that Flag in the dust 5 years ago danced under it
tonight, could not help but respect it, although it was verry
Mortifying to some of them. Bayonets taught them a lesson.

Sunday, September 10, 1865

had a little shottish last night. Embarked on Bd. Str. Magnolia
for Mobile where I arrived 9 P.M. found most of the men in
good health & all gaiety. Sergt. Sheeks & I walked out to the
cemeteries find great taste displayed.[49] visit the old Fortifications further out. find them numerous & strong in comdg. positions etc.

Monday 11

drew clothing, Medicines, and Rations. Embarked on Bd. Stmr.
Zephyr at 3 P.M. accompanied by T. H. Roseberry Sergt. Maj.
21" Mo. I.V.V.[50] arrived at East Pascagoula 9 in Evening. found
an Odr. there ordering us Co. "G" to rejoin our Regt. at Mobile
without delay. glad of it. while I was gone Frog-Eater ordered
Stoughton and Co. to leave the Hotel and Qr. in Tents. Stoughton refuses to go. consequently is placed in arrest.

Tuesday 12

Frog Eater rec'd orders to report with his command to New

[49] Both Union and Confederate dead were buried on the outskirts of
Mobile.
[50] The *Zephyr* was a troop transport that had operated on the Mississippi
River and along the Gulf coast during the war. She had been battered by
neutral storms and hostile cannons on several occasions.

Orleans. *dog Eat dog*. Issued clothing and make preparations to Embark on first Steamer for Mobile Ala. to rejoin our Regiment. one thing certain we will not have a Negro Comdr. to Tyranize over us when we get there. I think a change will be for the better.

Wednesday, September 13, 1865

Rained all the Afternoon but not withstanding we mooved Evrything down to the Wharf no Steamer came. went out in town in the Evening with some friends had a real nice Ball, the Col. Asked our Violinists to play for him. could not see it. all went Merry as a Marriage Bell.

Thursday 14

lay on the Peer all day in the Evening a Boat came and we began to think we was going to get off, but lo, the capt. had a special order to take the Negro Troops and no others, so we was merry again, the Nigs worked hard all night loading their supplies, while the Col. was mutched depressed to think he had to go first.

Friday 15

Kinkeys started this Morning at daylight. about ten Oclock the Zephyr arrived and we Embarked for Mobile at which place we arrived at the camp of the Regt. about 10 oclock at Night. S. Snyder and Cp[l.] James Joined us on the boat.[51] Boys are all on a protracted drunk & have been all day Capt. Included.

[51] Private Sanford Snyder, a tall, youthful veteran, and Corporal Amos James.

Saturday, September 16, 1865

busied ourselves in arrangeing a Camp & makeing ourselves as comfortable as possible. Companies "H" & "I" start from the camp for some special duty destination unknown to us at present. my health is already improoveing and I feel much better.

Sunday 17

have our camp verry nicely constructed, does not look so much like home as our Hotel. Surg. Roberts, Capt. Tracy, and Lt. Schram of 21" Mo. is aded to our Mess.[52] quite a family of us now. walked out to the cemeteries saw some splendid specimens of Architecture. also visited the soldiers Grave Yard, U.S. and C.S.[53]

Monday 18

went to town to try and get my commutation had no vouchers and could not get it. came home & made them out. John

[52] Major Abel C. Roberts, regimental surgeon, remained with the mess until October 28. His military career ended soon, but he remained active in veterans' affairs. In 1897–1899 he served as president of the 21st Missouri Regiment Infantry Veteran Volunteer Association. He died in 1901 in Fort Madison, Iowa. Captain Alexander F. Tracy of Company F soon resigned from the army. (See entry for September 21.) Lieutenant Isaac C. Schram, who had been promoted from first sergeant in May, 1864, was soon promoted again. (See entry for October 27.)

[53] Magnolia Cemetery was located in the western outskirts of Mobile. More than a thousand Confederate dead rested in its southeastern corner, and its southwestern corner held the Union troops who had fallen at Fort Blakely. Many prominent residents of Mobile were buried in Magnolia Cemetery, which later received the body of Braxton Bragg, a former Confederate general.

Springer returned from Pascagoula where he was left when we came way. walked through alone in 36 hours a distance of 48 Miles. Verry well done for an old man.[54] Quite a forced March.

Tuesday, September 19, 1865

Went to C.S. Office drew my commutation, went to Q.M. Dept. on Business.[55] was kept Busy the rest of the day makeing out charges and Specifications, Makeing Out Dec. Rolls and copying Orders etc. had a fine shower this Morn, and an other this Evening[.] several of Men are getting sick.

Wednesday 20

put in my time writing out Vouchers for the men to collect commuta[t]ion of rations on Old Furloughs. men are much disatisfied by being Kept in Service, and gieveing way to disipation in all manners, Capt. is quite sick. *Eat tomuch distilled corn.*

Thursday 21

Capt. Tracy Co. "F" and Lieut. Murry Co. "D" receive their Resignation Paper duly signed and Approoved will start home

[54] Private John Springer volunteered in June, 1861, at the age of 45. A former laborer, he served faithfully throughout the war, participating in many bloody battles. Though old enough to be Woodruff's father, Springer soldiered with the best of his youthful comrades, holding his own on every occasion.

[55] Both the Commissary of Subsistence Office and the Quartermaster Department were frequently contacted by Woodruff.

in a few days.[56] The same old story with me, sit at the old Desk
all day long and half of the night. no extra pay for it either.
I'm tired of it.

Friday, September 22, 1865

no change in the Programme only that I lay aside loosse papers
and pick up a New Descriptive Book, writing out Milty. History of Co. will take me some days to finish it. take a walk in
the city to settle my supper. Music greets my Ears on all corners,
and lovely Females. feel like possessing their charms, but resolve not to do it. have a finer Point in view.

Saturday 23

Rained without intermission all day. Evrything and Evrybody
is wet, impossible to Keep dry in Shelter Tents during such
rains.[57] Sergt. Butcher returns from Furlough, tells me that
Carrie is sick. I can but doubt him, Knowing that such a thing
is not impossible, I pitty Lidie, Marred of her pleasures so soon.

Sunday 24

continues to rain rain rain the livelong day. I had made up my

56 Both Captain Alexander F. Tracy, mentioned previously, and Second
Lieutenant Charles C. Morrey submitted their resignations on August 29.

57 By the middle of 1862 the standard field tent for Union troops was the
shelter or "dog" tent. This two-man "home" was constructed by buttoning
together the half-shelters carried by the occupants as standard equipment
and stretching them over a horizontal pole held in place by two upright
sticks or muskets with fixed bayonets. The ends were either left open or
draped with blankets. Very unpopular at first, these little tents proved their
worth in many rugged campaigns. The modern army's pup tent is the direct
descendent of the old dog tent.

mind to go to Church & see if there was not some attraction
there or something to drive dull care away. could not go on
acc't of the rain. continued reflection on the report of my absent
loved ones Illness forces the conviction that its true, the only
gratification left me is to write to her.

Monday, September 25, 1865

The Sun arose clear and bright. The day is beautiful and the
pleasant breeze from the North seems to say Toil on yet awhile,
and Ere long thou shalt be returned with honor to thy home
where friends and true love awaits with pleasure to welcome
Thee. work at Co. Descriptive Book and make out Vouchers
for Commutation for Sergt. Butcher.

Tuesday 26

I was awakened last Night and quite Enchanted at hearing a
Band discou[r]sing a lovely Serenade in the city, they were playing one of those lively Enchanting Melodies that never fails to
arouse the warmest Sympathy of the Soul; Pvt. C. McMichael
returned from Furlough.

Wednesday 27

General Inspection came off to day, the first One we have had
in our Regt. since the Rebellion *smashed.* made Application for
Furloughs for Corpl. Church, & Pvts. Clark and Bishop.[58] I

58 Private Abraham J. Clark was mentioned previously. (See entry for
July 29.) Private Mordica Bishop, a 40-year-old farmer, did not enlist until
the spring of 1864. He saw a good deal of combat, but he lacked the experience of many of his younger comrades, veterans like Corporal George S.
Church. These men left for home on October 2, returned on October 31,
and were reimbursed for rations on November 6. (See entries for these
dates.)

went to the city where I met some old chums and we got on a
regular Bender-run, the first time *I've* been *on it,* in a long
time.

Thursday, September 28, 1865

sleep verry late this morning, feel somewhat the worse for my
spree, drank Lagre Beer principally & that generally acts twice
on a fellow, so you can imagine me drunker to day than when
I lay down last night. & I'll leave you to follow in your Imagination how I got rid of it, "the Beer I mean" 'twas better distilled
when I was done with it, than when I began be assurred.

Friday 29

feel mutch better this morning, go to the city after the Mail get
none. make out Estimate for C.C. & G.E. for month of Oct. also
Invoices & Receipts for C. & G.E. turned over to Q.M. this
day.[59] go to the city again in the Evening in co. with the Lt.
get an Oyster Stew for 50 cts. apiece thats really Pallatable. my
Physical condition feels much revived after it.

Saturday 30

make out Monthly Return of Co., Return of Deserters, & Quarterly Return of Deceased Soldiers. spend a few hours writing
out the History of Co. that has been so troublesome to me of
late. The 14" Wis. I.V.V. camp adjoining ours received Orders

59 "C. & G.E." meant Camp and Garrison Equipage, slightly less com-
plicated than the previously mentioned "C. C. and G. E.," Clothing, Camp
and Garrison Equipage.

to make out their Muster-Out Rolls at Once.[60] I presume our turn will come next as we are the only Vol. Regt. left in the place.

Sunday, October 1, 1865

busied myself most of the day writing letters, in the Evening two men of Co. "F" came in to camp looking as though had just returned from a hard fought Battle & were looking for a Surg. to dress their Wounds. one with a gastly wound in left side near the heart. The other in rigt. arm, Effect of Negroes steel.

Monday 2

Put in the day at the Descriptive Book, and in makeing out Estimate for Clothing Camp and Garrison Equipage, and Invoices of C & G. E to Lt M. N. Sinnett A.R.Q.M. 21" Mo. Infty. Vet. Vols.[61] Corpl. C. & two Men start home on Furlough of 30 ds.[62]

Tuesday 3

Completed Co. History to present date, & Estimate for C.C. & G.E. for month of Oct. 1865. Co. Signed June Rolls for four

[60] The 14th Wisconsin Infantry Veteran Volunteer Regiment, organized early in 1862, paid a high price for its wartime glory: 122 men killed in action and another 197 dead of disease. It served with the 21st Missouri in the operations against Mobile at the end of the war, including the last assault on Fort Blakely. The 14th Wisconsin was mustered out of service on October 9, 1865.

[61] First Lieutenant Martin N. Sinnott of Company E was Acting Regimental Quartermaster.

[62] See footnote 58.

months pay, say we will get it in a day or two. doubtful in my case if I get any or not as I was not present at Muster detained in Hosp. by reason of Wound.

Wednesday, October 4, 1865

Make out clothing Schedules for Month of September 1865. write out request to have Corpl. L. reduced to ranks for *drunkenness, Dispt.* to *C.O.* etc. Mc gets in a fight over a game with one of Co. "E" & gets badly whiped.[63] is bruised in head & face with *Shelalah* in a shocking manner.

Thursday 5

2 Lt. 1 Sergt. I Corpl. & 15 Privts. are detailed to guard Prison in the city, 1 Privt. detailed as Mounted Orderly. our Co. is smaller now than it Ever was, over ½ is absent. drew *Wedge Tents* & worked hard all day in remoddleing Camp and makeing ourselves as comfortable as possible for Winter Qrs. as we suppose.[64]

Friday 6

perhaps I had better introduce Stoughton, as he has been lay-

[63] Corporal L., who suddenly made private again, is unidentifiable. The trooper so badly clubbed by a member of Company E may well have been Private (formerly Sergeant) Charles McMichael, who had just returned from leave on September 26. (See note 41.)

[64] The wedge or "A" tent looked like an inverted V in front. Essentially it was a piece of canvas stretched over a horizontal bar and staked to the ground on both sides, with extensions at both ends for closing. The interior normally accommodated four men. A tall trooper could not stand erect, and the farther from the ridge pole he stood, the more he had to stoop. There was very little room for furnishings.

ing in obscurity for a long time. he has been going it about the same old stile Ever since we came here. more or less of the "Esence" passes his black throat evry day. he is never empty & never draws a sober breath. has not been heard of for 24 hours back. copy 2 Months Reports 3 times[.] I have copied them & they are now permanent.

Saturday, October 7, 1865

Completed the mooveing of Camp & as for myself I am going to resign my self calmly to sweet contentment, & await the Will of Uncle Sam-u-e-l to muster me out. she can not get rid of me now until she gives me an honorable Discharge. copied an other Months Morning reports. Stoughton made his appearance about 10 OK. nearer Empty than he has been for a long time.

Sunday 8

Lieut. Harris is brougt out from the city to Regtl. Hosp. verry sick with Diarrhoea. take a walk in the Evening with some friends to the Cemeteries where I find can be seen on the Sabbath the Elite of the city decorating the Tombs of the sacred dead with wreaths of Flowers.

Monday 9

the Co. is relieved from further duty in the city by reason of Lts sickness, not able to comd. them. was paid four months pay & one Inst. Bounty.[65] All are Merry, and many drunk. Capt.

65 When Woodruff reenlisted early in 1864, he received a 30-day furlough and a four-hundred-dollar bounty that was paid not in a lump sum but in periodic fifty-dollar installments.

goes to the city and returns verry sick. Surg. considers his recovery doubtful.

Tuesday, October 10, 1865

Spent the day in collecting & paying off old accounts etc. etc. As near as I can learn there was about 14 commissions re'cd. in the 21" capt. Blackburn as Major, Lt. Allen as Capt, Lt. Harris as 1" Lieut. & T. H. Roseberry Sergt. Major as 2" Lieut. of Co. "G" none of the above named can Muster at present dont Know as they ever will.[66]

Wednesday 11

went to Market Early got a steak for Breakfast. went to the City & Expressed the Lt.['s] Money for him. wrote a letter to his wife, is no better. Capt. is improoveing. Various rumors of Muster Out, learned of Pvt. I. Longcor who has been absent for some time, is in jail in city, by Civil authority.

Thursday 12

Sanford Snyder is taken sick verry suddenly supposed to have congestive chill. Capt. is geting quite stout again is able to walk round[.] Lt. H. is getting worse. J.H.D. is relieved from Det. Ser. P. Pitts relieved for drunkeness.[67] 1 Btln. of Regulars Arrives in city. Enter[t]a[i]n a strong hope of going home soon.

[66] Officially, these promotions were made on September 30. All of the officers have been previously mentioned except Captain Daniel R. Allen, another combat veteran, who was soon appointed Assistant Provost Marshal in Mobile.

[67] Private John H. Denney, a farmer who saw much action in only fifteen months of wartime duty, was relieved from detached service. Private Peter Pitts was in trouble again on October 22.

Friday, October 13, 1865

Gave two of the men a pass, went to the city and abused it and consequently was arrested and lodged in Prison for safe Keeping till morning. busied myself most of the day Issueing clothing, sick men are all improoveing, save Lt. H. who continues quite feeble.

Saturday 14

The two men who was arrested yesterday, was released to day & restored to Co. on written request to P.M. & by the way, we Enjoyed a hearty laugh over their Misfortunes & at their Expense.[68] went to Dist. Hd. Qrs. and got My pass approoved. Enjoyed an agreeable walk in the city.

Sunday 15

Witnessed a Masonic Burial of Lt. Burns 15" U.S.I. died on the night of the 13" of Whiskey on the Brain.[69] learned of 2 Members of 77" O.V.V.I. being in the city, went to look for them,

[68] The two troopers released by the provost marshal are never identified.
[69] George H. Burns, a Pennsylvanian, enlisted early in the war and served with distinction. He was promoted rapidly and, following a fine performance in the bloody battle of Murfreesboro in December, 1862, he was breveted captain. His unit, the 15th United States Infantry Regiment (Regular Army), was first organized in West Virginia in 1861. It saw action in many battles, including Shiloh, Murfreesboro, and Chattanooga, and suffered heavy losses—134 men killed in action, another 229 dead of various diseases. Friction soon developed between this veteran unit of regulars and the seasoned volunteers of the 21st Missouri. (See entries for December 7 and 14.)

could not find them.[70] one of Co. "G" comes in after retreat
& tatoo is over, minus his coat & Boots. was *Mugged* by the
Regulars in the Suburbs & lost them.

Monday, October 16, 1865

wrote request to the Adjutant to have Corporal Morris reduced
to the Ranks for drunkeness & disorderly conduct.[71] 3 men
are detailed to Guard Paymaster through the country while he
pays absent companies. Capt. has quite recovered & looks like
a new man. Lt. H. is slowly recovering, walks out some.

Tuesday 17

went to the city for supplies for Mess. Men are all geting the
Blues, tis Enough to give it to one. Men that came of[f] duty
this morning, I had to detail again tonight. 3 of the men are
sick with chills & Fever. The boys brought out their *Ladies*
last night & had a dance: "A good thing" I can not imply the
term *Ladies* in the sense it is comonly used. "see Note 1"
January." Note 1" in journal of Oct. 17" I refered you to note
1" January. I will not discuss the point here in way I would
under other circumstances, but merely change the programme.
This Evening two or three small girls 10 or twelve years of age

[70] The 77th Ohio Veteran Volunteer Infantry Regiment was organized
at Marietta, the capital of Woodruff's home county. Obviously, many boy-
hood friends were in this unit. The 77th had plenty of combat experience,
including the dubious distinction of being captured virtually as a unit at
Marks' Mills, Arkansas, on April 25, 1864. Exchanged in February, 1865, the
77th participated in the final assault on Mobile without suffering any
losses. Overall, it lost 70 men in combat and 210 to disease. The 77th was
soon transferred to Texas, where it was mustered out in March, 1866.

[71] Joseph Morris, another young veteran, appears again in the entries
for October 26 and 30—as a private, not a corporal.

came out on the balcony of a dwelling situated not more than a
stone's throw from our camp and displayed the Rebel Flag.
Huzaing for the *Red White & Red*.[72] A Collored Cook in the
yard after Water droped a remark, when the Madam appeared
with a saucy rebuke & insults to all *Yanks,* saying "they" (the
south was not whiped) & if they got a chance would raise again.
Such I know to be the prevailing sentiments throughout the
South. One can walk the streets any night in the city here &
hear the Ladies singing & playing the Bonnie Blue Flag & other
Treasonable airs,[73] & we are evry day subject in the camp or
out of it, to the insults & tantalizeing boasts and that right in
presence of the authorities, and dare not resist it. Go where you
will & you will hear barefaced Treason utered in the strongest
terms, even the Public Press does not hesitate to pitch its vile
rebukes right into the teeth of the authorities & express sentiments that three years ago would have suppressed any Public
Paper in Chicago, Cincinnatti, or New York city, & yet 'tis not
noticed. All is well and the[y] is reassuming Loyal measures & the
Government is assured of its Allegiance to that Govt. & the
Union and its all true (in a Horn with both ends open) "and I
believe I can see it." There is not 9 out of 10 of these so called
"Whiped" traitors that I would trust until I saw the rope ap-
plied to their Necks, then I would only have Faith in the
quality of the rope. & here we see them evry day restored to all
their former rights & privalidges, put in office and other responsible positions in the North as well as South where the

[72] The rebels fought under a conglomeration of local, state, and Confederate banners. The *"Red White & Red"* could have referred to either
the first or last national Confederate flag, both of which had at least a
partial red-white-red pattern.
[73] "The Bonnie Blue Flag" was one of the Confederacy's favorite patriotic
songs. Henry Macarthy wrote the words, and Valentine Vousden adapted the
music from an old Irish song. The flag itself was composed of a white star
in the middle of a field of dark blue.

true patriot and loveing defender of his country and the only self deserving men of our country, is refused. I will mention one little case that will Illustrate the fact, of the superintendent of the U. S. Military Telegraph at New Orleans who was tinctured with Treason, who had a discharged Soldier employed as chief clerk. The Supt. met with an old acquaintance who had Served during the War in the Rebel Army, & was now out of employment, whom he hires & advances the wages two dollars above the other man & turns him off.[74] This is Justice, Oh yes, we must help the South, love and forgive them. I can never do it only in the way I have been dooing for the last four years & I presume some of them have realized that love to the fullest extent during that period. if not, 'twas not my fault.

Wednesday 18

received Orders to prepare for genl. Inspection at 10. o ck. all in readiness but looks so stormy it is defered till the Morrow. Go to the city with Holmes the Suttler who gets a Kegg of Beer and we have a splendid time, make arrangements to go on a Regular Bum in the Evening, but the duties in camp prevent it.

[74] This incident occurred during Mayor Hugh Kennedy's administration in New Orleans. Kennedy was accused of favoring former rebels in his appointments, and he was even briefly removed from office in May, 1865 by General S. A. Hurlbut. However, he was reinstated on June 9, 1865 and served until the following March, when he was succeeded by John T. Monroe, who was even more "pro-Southern." Monroe was briefly removed from office by General Edward R. S. Canby, but he finally resumed his post on May 11 and served for a year. During Monroe's administration city police and other armed whites killed and wounded many Negroes and their white sympathizers in a bloody riot that shocked and angered the North. Sergeant Woodruff was obviously not the only Union soldier who hated to see "traitors" replace "patriots" in positions of prestige and power in the South.

Thursday, October 19, 1865

All is bustle in the camp this Morning geting ready for the Inspection. Maj. Clapp arrives at Ten.[75] The Battallion is so small they form them all in one Company dose not make a good one then. tis soon over and all is going off in the same old stile and that is not smooth by odds.

Friday 20

some of the men have been on duty for 3 days and I am compelled to detail them again to day. I. W. Figgans, H. S. Bostwick & J. K. P. Wilson all of my Co. are arrested & confined for the reason that 2 horses disappeared from Hd.Qrs. while they were on duty there Guarding them, and they can not account for them.[76] make out returns of Qr. Mr. Stores.

Saturday 21

Get an ambulance & go to the city to Market for Sunday. On our way down Dauphine St. came in contact with a Dray drove by a small Negro boy who attempts to make the crossing in our front while we are traveling at nearly R.R. time.[77] The con-

[75] Probably Major Dexter E. Clapp of the 38th United States Colored Infantry.

[76] Private Thomas W. Figgins was a tall, tough veteran, and Privates James K. P. Wilson and Henry S. Bostwick had also seen much combat, though they had served in the wartime army only a little over a year. Bostwick was in trouble again on November 17.

[77] Dauphin Street was originally planned and named in 1711 by Governor Bienville. One of the few main streets to retain its original French name, it ran from the western outskirts into the heart of the city. Sergeant Woodruff's speeding ambulance wagon doubtless had the "right of way" over the luckless cart emerging from a side street.

sequence is when Sambo has found himself, he is standing on
the sidewalk showing his Ivorys to the bottom of his dray
which is bottom up leaning against a Dry goods Establishment
on the oposite side of the street.

Sunday, October 22, 1865

Get Orders from Hd. Quarters to Put Private Peter Pitts on
Extra duty for Shirking duty yesterday, has been on for Six days
in Succession. Go out on a spree with Sergts. Russell, Tulley,
Loona etc. etc. with whom I scraped an acquaintance belong
to the 15" U.S.I.[78] find them verry gentlemanly fellows, but
heavy on the Beer. real sports while greenbacks are at *Par*.

Monday 23

Murch[79] one of the detail of Guard at the Ord. Depot thinks
to amuse the party in the Evening at the Expense of an un-
suspecting citizen by burning Powder under their feet which
he Extracts from the stores he is guarding. he accordingly places
about 18 Hs. in a string across the street & touched off with a
Brand he as fate would have it not being aware of the danger
to himself was severely burn[e]d in the face & hands is now in
Hospital.   *see note 2 January.

Note 2" referred from 23" October

Some Gentlemen whom I judge to be insane has favored the

78 Unidentifiable.

79 A 33-year-old farmer, Chauncey Murch enlisted in January, 1864. Private Murch had seen enough combat to know the danger of playing with
gunpowder. (See entry for December 20.)

Col. with some verry strange letters, in one of them, they tell him, they will give him 20 days to Muster us out of the Service, if we are not out in that length of time they will find a piece of real estate for him not over two½ miles from this place.[80] They conclude by telling him if he chooses to answer to address any of the Company & his communication will be received, and *do not sign their name to it.* The Petition forwarded by the Offs. of the 21" to the Secty of War through his Excellency Gov. Fletcher to be Mustered out has been returned bearing endorsements of the diferent Officials.[81] Genl. Wood comdg. Dept. of Ala. says that all the Troops that can at present be spared from this Dept. has previously been ordered Mustered out.[82]

[80] The regimental commander at this time was Colonel Joseph G. Best. A native of Ireland, Best was a 24-year-old clerk when the war began, and he soon enlisted in the ranks. Promotion followed promotion, and by the summer of 1862 he was a captain. By the end of the war he was a major. He became a full colonel on September 30, 1865.

[81] Thomas Clement Fletcher was governor of Missouri from January, 1865 until January, 1869. Before the war he opposed slavery, and in 1856 he joined the nascent Republican Party. He supported Lincoln at the Chicago convention; and, when war came, he quickly enlisted in the Union forces. As colonel of the 31st Missouri Infantry, he was wounded and captured at Chickasaw Bayou, but he was exchanged in time to witness the fall of Vicksburg. He fought at Chattanooga and in the Atlanta campaign, and he commanded the Union force that drove the rebels away from St. Louis in the spring of 1864. For his services he was breveted brigadier general—and nominated for the governorship by the Republicans. He was elected by a large majority in 1864 and easily reelected in 1866. After retiring from politics, Fletcher practiced law, first in St. Louis and then in the nation's capital, until his death in 1899.

[82] Major General Thomas John Wood, a regular from Kentucky, was twice wounded while compiling an enviable combat record in some of the bloodiest battles of the Civil War. His swift obedience to an erroneous order paved the way for rebel victory at Cickamauga, but, justly, he was not blamed for the stupidity of a superior officer. In the latter stages of the conflict his division performed brilliantly at Missionary Ridge, Atlanta, and Nashville. After the war he won a reputation as a humane, lenient occupation officer. Partially disabled by wartime wounds, he was retired in June, 1868, but he lived until 1906 and was the last survivor of the West Point class of 1845.

That seals our doom & we will certainly have to serve the rest
of the Winter.

Tuesday 24

make out Schedules of C.C. and G.E. for the Issue in fore part
of the Month. The Col. has some difficulty with a conscript of
Co. "A" whom he suspects of writing the Misterious letter,
& sends him to Military Prison in the city. dont Know his real
name is Known by the name of Big *Sandy* throughout the camp.

Wednesday, October 25, 1865

passing through the city I saw a person a "Lewd Woman"
whom I supposed to be trying to drive the front door through
the oposite side of the House piece at a time by the way she
made splinters fly with an Ax. & the Language Expressed by
her & others was too disgusting for mortal Erars to hear, let
alone Express them.

Thursday 26

Pvt. R. Carr returns from Hospl. where he has been since 1"
of March.[83] Pvt. Jos. Morris is detailed as Mounted Orderly
at U. S. M. Telph. office. Make out Invoices and recpts. of
Camp and G. E. and Monthly Returns of C. & G.E. for Lt.

---

[83] Private Richard Carr, a short, blond Irishman, joined the Union army
in 1861 at the age of 40. Captured at Shiloh, he was exchanged in time to
see much further combat. A lifetime of farming made him tough enough
to soldier with his younger comrades.

Harris pertain[in]g to Military Prison in Mobile. Lt. H. has returned from Hospl. still quite feeble.

Friday 27

The Officers were all out on the Shell Road to witness the
Races going off there, Capts. B. & S. hire a horse & carriage
from Stables to attend the scenes.[84] The horse is rather un-
managable & by the way come in contact with a Dray & the
carriage is smashed consequently they tie the horse to an ambulance & change the programme entire.

Saturday, October 28, 1865

Dr. Roberts ceases to be member of Mess & goes to board with
his family who arrived this Morning. begin a Muster Roll for
the last two Months preprareatory to Muster for pay the last of
this [month]. some gent in on the News Orders Pvt. S. to "stand
and deliver,["] S gets the beter of him, Knocks him down &
transfers him to the patrolls.[85]

Sunday 29

went out in the city to see the fashions. A *Lady* siting in her
door as I passed accosted me with "hallow" come back & talk
to a feller, you yanks grow so d——d tall, yes, we are long poles,
"give a feller a chaw tobacker, dont use the weed, "damned

84 Captain Edward K. Blackburn had just been promoted to major, and
Captain Isaac C. Schram had also just been promoted.
85 Probably Private Sanford Snyder.

cold,d'ye Know where I could get a caw tobacker, yes, where you got your *Whiskey* "Exit"

Monday 30

Make out a Muster Roll all ready to Muster tomorrow. Make out Descriptive list of Jos. Morris. get orders to make out estimate for C.C. and G.E. for November. *dad* one of Natures comics goes to the city, takes too much of the O-be-Joyful, sidewalk flies up & strikes him in the face spoiling his "phiz" for him. Swore some one had "mugged him."

Tuesday, October 31, 1865

Mustered for pay. Corpl. Church & Privates Clark & Bishop returned in time to Muster. Settled Mess Accts. for the Month, Made out Monthly returns for Co. Suttlers & citizens get in a fight & Soldier Bucks & wins the day driveing the enemy off the field.

Wednesday, November 1

Make out Monthly Return of Deserters. by the way, we had none, so it was a short Job. Make out a Muster & Pay Roll complete. learned of one of our men "Mauck" being in Military prison for stealing Coton. was on Det. Service, had a "good thing"[86]

[86] Private Mathew Mauck was a 19-year-old veteran of one year of wartime service. He was far from the only occupation soldier looking for a "good thing," and he continued to get into trouble. (See entries for November 2 and 10, and December 6.)

Sergeant Woodruff's Diary

WEDNESDAY, SEPTEMBER 13, 1865.

Rained all the afternoon but not withstanding we moved everything down to the Wharf the Steamer came went out in town in the evening with some friends had a real nice Ball, the Col asked our Violinists to play for him. could not see it. all went Merry as a Marriage Bell

THURSDAY 14

lay on the Pier all day in the evening a Boat came and we began to think we was going to get off, but lo the capt. had a special order to take the Negro Troops & no others. as we was merry again, the Nigs worked hard all night loading their supplies, while the Col was much depressed to think he had to go first.

FRIDAY 15

Niskeys started this Morning at daylight. about ten oclock the Zephyr arrived and we embarked for Mobile at which place we arrived at the camp of the Regt. about 10 oclock at Night. S. Snyder & Ct. James joined us on the boat. Boys are all on a protracted drunk & have been all day Capt. included.

SATURDAY, SEPTEMBER 16, 1865.

busied ourselves in arranging our Camp & making ourselves as comfortable as possible. Companies B. & I start from the camp for some special duty destination unknown to us at present. my health is already improving and I feel much better.

SUNDAY 17

have our camp very nicely constructed, does not look so much like home as our Hotel. Surg. Roberts Capt. Tracy & Lt. Schram & Mrs. is added to our Mess. quite a family of us now walked out to the cemeteries saw some splendid specimens of Architecture. also visited the soldiers grave yard, W.A. & C.S.

MONDAY 18

went to Town to try and get my commutation had no re there and could not get it. came home & made them out. John Springer returned from Pascagoula where he was left when we came up. walked through alone in 36 hours a distance of 48 miles. very well done for a old man. quite a forced March

Sergeant Woodruff's Diary

TUESDAY, SEPTEMBER 19, 1865.

went to C. S. Office drew my commutations, went to Q. M. Dpt. on Business was kept Busy the rest of the day making out charges & Specifications. Making out Ord. Rolls & copying Orders &c. had a fine shower this morn. and an other this evening several of men are getting sick.

WEDNESDAY 20

put in my time writing out vouchers for the men to collect commutations of rations out alot furloughs. men are much disatisfied by being kept in Service and giving way to disipation in all manners. Capt. is quite sick. Eat to much distilled corn.

THURSDAY 21

Capt. Tracy Co. "F" & Lieut. Murry Co. "D". receive their Resignation Paper duly signed and Approoved will start home in a few days. the same old story with me. sit at the old Desk all day long & half of the night. no extra pay for it Either. I'm tired of it.

FRIDAY, SEPTEMBER 22, 1865.

no change in the Programme only that I lay aside Loose papers & pick up a New Discriptive Book. writing out Milty History of Co. will take me some days to finish it. take a walk in the city to settle my supper. Music greets my ears on all corners and lovely Females. feel like possessing their charms but resolve not to do it. have a firer point in view.

SATURDAY 23

Rained without intermission all day. everything and everybody is wet impossible to keep dry in Shelter Tents during such rains. Sergt. Butcher returns from Furlough. tells me that Carrie is sick. I can but doubt him. knowing that such a thing is not imposible. I pitty Lidie. Warned of her pleasures so soon.

SUNDAY 24

continues to rain. rain rain the livelong day. I had made up my mind to go to Church & see if there was not some attraction there or something to drive dull care away. could not go on acct. of the rain. continued reflection on the report of my absent loved one for-ces the conviction that its true. the only gratification left me is to write to her

Sergeant Woodruff's Diary

MONDAY, SEPTEMBER 25, 1865.

The Sun arose clear & bright. The day is beautiful and the pleasant breeze from the North Sun's do pray toil to yet awhile and ere long thou shalt be returned with honor to thy home where friends and true love await with pleasure to welcome Thee. work at Co. Description Book & make out Vouchers for Commutation for Sergt. Butcher.

TUESDAY 26

I was awakened last Night & quite enchanted at hearing a Band discoursing a lovely Serenade in the city. they were playing one of those lively enchanting Melodies that never fails to arouse the warmest Sympathy of the Soul. Pvt. C. McMichael returned from Furlough.

WEDNESDAY 27

General Inspection came off to day. the first One we have had in our Regt since the Rebellion smashed. made Application for Furloughs for Corpl. Church & Pvts. Clark and Bishop. I went to the city where I met some old chums & we got on a regular Bender-um. the first time I've been on it in a long time.

THURSDAY, SEPTEMBER 28, 1865.

sleep very late this morning feel somewhat the worse for my spree. drank Lager Beer principally & that generally acts twice on a fellow so you can imagine me drunker to day than when I lay down last night & I'll leave you to follow in your imagination how I got rid of it. the Beer I mean - twas better die filled when I was done with it. than when I began be assured.

FRIDAY 29

feel much better this morning. go to the city after the mail get none. make out estimate for C. C. & Q. E. for month of Oct. also Invoices & Receipts for C. & Q. B. turned over to Q.M. this day. go to the city again in the evening & co. with the Lt. get an Oyster Stew for 50 cts that was really Palatable. my Physical condition feels much revived after it.

SATURDAY 30

make out Monthly Return of Co. Return of Deserters. & Quarterly Return of Deceased Soldiers. spend a few hours writing out the History of Co. that has been so troublesome to me of late. the 14" Wis. I. Vol. camps adjoining ours received Orders to make out their Muster-out Rolls at Once. I presume our turn will come next as we are the only Vol Regt left in the place.

Sergeant Woodruff's Diary

SUNDAY, OCTOBER 1, 1865.

busied myself most of the day writing letters. in the evening two men of Co. "F." came in to camp looking as though had just returned from a hard fought Battle & were looking for a Surg. to dress their wounds. one with a gash wound in left side near the heart the other in rgt. arm. effect of Negroes steel.

MONDAY 2

hard in the day at the Descriptive Book. and in making out estimate for Clothing Camp and Garrison Equipage, and invoices of C & G. E. to Lt. W. M. Sinnett A. A. Q.M. 31st Wis. Infty. Vet Vols. Corpl. C. & two men start home on Furlough of 30 ds.

TUESDAY 3

Completed Co. History to present date. & estimate for C. & G. E. for month of Oct. 1865. Co. Signed pay Rolls for four months pay, say we will get it in a day or two. doubtful in my case if I get any or not as I was not present at Muster detained in Hosp. by reason of wound.

WEDNESDAY, OCTOBER 4, 1865.

make out clothing Schedules for month of September 1865. write out request to have Corpl. L. reduced to ranks for drunkeness. Desp. to C. O. &c. Mc guts in a fight over a game with one of Co. "D." & gets badly whiped. is bruised in head & face with Shelalah in a shocking manner.

THURSDAY 5

2 Lt. 1 Sergt. 1 Corpl. & 15 Privts. are detailed to Guard Prison in the city. 1 Prvt. detailed as Mounted Orderly. our Co. is smaller now than it ever was over ½ is absent. drew Wedge Tents & worked hard all day in remodelling Camp. and making ourselves as comfortable as possible for Winter & as we suppose

FRIDAY 6

perhaps I had better introduce Stoughton, as he has been laying in obscurity for a long time. he has been going it about the same old style ever since we came here more or less of the "Essence" papers his black throat every day. he is never empty & never draws a sober breath. has not been heard of for 24 hours back. copy 3 months Reports 3 times I have copied them & they are no permanent

Thursday 2

wrote application for Furloughs for Corpl. Sherrick & Privates
Wm. Anderson & Sam. Davalt.[87] work a few hours on Pay
Rolls. sets rain so hard I have to postpone business. Mauck
turns States Evidence against his comrad[e]s & gets out of Prison, he will cheat the gallows of its just dues, some day, has not
far to go.

Friday, November 3, 1865

Completed Muster & Pay Rolls by working verry late. Lt. H.
is geting quite well. Capt. falling back on his old Friend again.
Stoughton lost his Father lately, several men are sick. some
taken verry suddenly of late. Murch[']s burn is geting beter, had
lost all hopes of him.

Saturday 4

went with the Capt. to the Theater. The first time for me in
Mobile. it was to be the last night of Frank Drew the great
commedian of the day. performance concluded with "Dick
Turpin & Tom King" on the "high way"[.][88] Actors read,
great applause from all circles.

[87] Corporal Joseph Sherrick, Private William Anderson, and Private
Samuel Devault all had about a year of wartime service. They actually left
on leave on November 6, but only two of the three got back on time. (See
entries for December 5 and 6.)

[88] Frank Drew was the brother of the more famous John Drew, the Irish
comedian who had died in 1862 at the age of 34. Frank offered a varied
repertoire to large, enthusiastic audiences in Mobile and was lauded by the
local press. He left for Philadelphia following the Saturday performance.
Frank Drew continued to perform for many years, and by the time of his
death at the age of 75 he had acted in more than a thousand different plays.

Sunday 5

lodged at the "Battle House" last night.[89] some of our fast young men was arrested yesterday for passing counterfeit Money. get lodging at Milty. Prison "free bill". All is quiet to day save the Muster out feever, creates quite an Excitement where tis agitated. Verry cold for this climate. think of Winter Qrs.

Monday, November 6, 1865

wrote out a request to Capt. Thos. Thompson, Asst. Adjt. Genl. Dist. of Mobile, to have Pvt. S. Snyder relieved from Special duty in P.O. Dept. & returned to Co.[90] Corpl. Sherrick, Pvts. S. Davalt & Wm. Anderson start North on Furlough. make out Vouchers for Corpl. Church & Pvts. A.J. Clark & M. Bishop to collect commutation of rations while on Furlough.

Tuesday 7

Officers Organized Ball Club last night. I was choosen as a member, had a fine game to day. Yesterday the Sixth was Election day in this State.   * see Note 3 Jan.

Note 3. refered from 7 November

There was a general election held throughout the State of Ala.

[89] The first Battle House opened in 1852, and for half a century it was a prominent American hotel. Five stories high, with accommodations for 300 guests, it was the city's finest hotel, famous for its service and its atmosphere.

[90] Despite the proper request to Captain Thomas Thompson, the assistant adjutant general, Private Sanford Snyder was not relieved immediately. (See entry for November 8.)

yesterday to send Representatives to Congress & returns are
not in yet. I have been so busy [to]day did not read the paper,
don't Know how the Election went in the city or what transpired, although from hearsay, I think it went off verry peace-
able considering. heard of Several drunken rows which are verry
comon on election days, & to tell the truth, most any day in a
southern city like Mobile. One man was up before the Provost
Martial this Morning, the 7" Nov., for Stabing an other with a
Knife so badly that he is not Expected to Live. The offender is
being held in custody til a change for better or worse is mani-
fest. There was an Order Issued to Keep all Soldiers in camp
during the day, which I think was verry beneficial from the fact
that Politicians of either side can not say, that the Election in
Mobile was controled by Yankee Bayonets, as they have in Virginia and Elsewhere. if they have not elected *Loyal* candidates,
their Treachery is confirmed by their own Voice as well as
deeds.[91] By the way, I have just learned of a Capt. .... of the
86" U.S.C.I. being shot in a house of Ill-fame in the city last
evening.[92] The election will be a good "come off" for him
of course. I am verry anxious indeed to hear the Returns of
the Election thinking it will have some bearing in regard to the

[91] The winning candidate in the Mobile congressional district was C. C.
Langdon. A northerner by birth and a former Whig, he had backed the
Bell–Everett ticket in the presidential election of 1860, and in 1861, as a
member of the Alabama legislature, he had opposed secession. When war
came, he had supported his state and the Confederacy. Thus Langdon was
a prewar "conservative" who reluctantly joined his people in rebellion.
Join he did, however, and in Woodruff's view he would be simply another
traitor. Four of the five other Alabama congressmen-elect were former Whigs
who also had rebelled reluctantly. Like Woodruff, Congress made no distinction between reluctant and eager rebels. Modern historians still quarrel
over this distinction.

[92] The 14th Regiment Infantry, Corps de Afrique, was organized at New
Orleans in August, 1863. After eight months of routine garrison duty, the
unit was renamed the 86th United States Colored Infantry. Further non-
combat assignments followed until the last weeks of the war, when the 86th
participated in the siege and capture of Fort Blakely. After a year of occupation duty along the Gulf coast, the regiment was mustered out.

Mustering out of the troops in this Dept. There is a verry good prospect at present for us to serve our time out, at least to serve til the coming summer. Jas. Roseberry & "speckled Dick" & others got in a Row in the city.[93] Dick was severely cut in right hand, Roseberry so badly bruised as to be blind & bedfast tonight. a crowd has gone to the city for sweet revenge.

Wednesday 8

Completed Monthly Returns of C.C. & G.E. for Month of Sept. went out to play a game of Ball, bursted ball & spoiled the fun. Lt. Hs leave of A. came back approoved will start home in a few days. request to relieve S.S. came back disapprooved. A.A.G. relieved, had to write out an other.[94] weather fine. all quiet on the Ala.

Thursday, November 9, 1865

Capts. Arthur & Hammond C.S. at Mobile Ala. came out to play a game of ball.[95] had a real good game, fine amusement & good exorcise. Lt. Rees was also present.[96] transmited Return

93 Private James Roseberry, another young veteran, had been transferred to Company I of the 21st Missouri. "speckled Dick" is unidentifiable. Roseberry had a more profitable adventure on December 4.

94 See note 90.

95 Captain Walter C. Arthur of Michigan and Captain Barnabas B. Hammond, a New Yorker, were assigned to the Commissary of Subsistence in Mobile.

96 First Lieutenant Richard Rees joined the 16th Illinois Volunteer Infantry Regiment in May, 1861 as a private. He received a series of rapid promotions, and in April, 1862 he was made a second lieutenant in the 21st Missouri. He was mustered out on April 19, 1866 but soon reenlisted and served another few years before finally terminating his army career.

of C.C. & G.E. to Qr. Mr. Genl. Wash'tn D.C. soldiers ordered to pull off citizens clothing. creates quite a sensasion with some.

Friday 10

did not play to day. all are tired & sore from too much exorcise yesterday. make out return of C.C. & G.E. for month of Oct. all square to date, in that line. Glessner & Mauck from too free indulgence in Sod-corn come to blows. Are confined till sobered off [.] Capt. reeling from Effects of the same orders charges prefered for drunkeness, etc.

Saturday 11

Witnessed Schedules and transmited return of C.C. & G.E. for oct. to Qr. Mr. Genl. Lt. Harris goes North on 20 days leave of absence. went to Q.M. Office C[lothing] Dept. & Exchanged pr. of Trowsers. went to the city and drank some Beer and p[l]ayed a few games of Dominoe.   * see Note 4. January.

Note 4. refered from Nov. 11"

On my return from the city I saw quite a crowd collected on the corner near the suttlers tent, turning my steps thither, I found Capts. Arthur and Hammond present with a couple of scrub horses which they were going to run against Maj. Mc-Gonigle's.[97] The proposed race course was about a mile distant near the Fortifications, a black Boy was mounted on scrub for

97 Major Henry McGonigle was officially promoted to lieutenant colonel on September 30, 1865.

rider. Scrub supposeing all was in readiness & the track clear
set off at full speed, running round 2 squares with the juvenile
who was unable to controll him, comeing out the starting point
& dumping Nig in the ditch ran over the stewards tent tearing
a frightful hole in it, large enough for horse rider & all to go
through with ease, & ran an other round of a mile where he was
caught & brought back snorting with head & tail up, to the
great delight of the amused spectators. Sambo, although not
injured by his fall, was rather loth to mount the fiery steed
again. Consequently C. C. Davis of my Co. who by the way is
possessed of more than one mans allowance of legs & feet, & is
verry clumsy make the best of him but is of a bold darring
spirit on such occasions was selected to ride the scrub. he thought
to play a wise part however by not mounting till he got to the
starting point. All now set out for the scene of action where arrived near sunset. Judges on the stand[,] track clear[,] riders up,
signal given and away they go. Maj. gets a little the start &
scrub runs round him in the rear & takes the other side of the
track, half a mile heat & Major wins the race. Scrub it appears
was not content with this short heat, but dashes on, after running 1½ miles he gets tired of burthen & tosses him over a Stake
& rider fence into a corn field, & the last we heard from scrub
he had mounted the Barricades & was going at lightning speed
to parts unknown. The suposition is, that he being tired of
City life & the monotonies thereof has bid adieu to his war-
fareing friends, and gone to seek a Solitary abode in the quiet
of the Interior. Davis walked to camp & was not thought to be
seriously injured, but at this late hour 10 oclock complains of
being verry stiff & sore. if we have an other race, I will let you
Know. I almost forgot to mention a party discovered to be connected with a gang of counterfeiters, who was Nov. 1" discovered to have immense amounts of counterfeit Greenbacks
in their possession. The amount in various bills up to date of

discovery when traced out amounted to several hundred dollars. J. Barnes & two Sexton Brothers of Cos. "E" & "D" was arrested & confined in Military Prison. Tom Hobson was implicated in trio, but got wind of what was in store for him & Deserted.[98] He has been Color Sergeant of the regt. for some months, has always been a noted rascal, at the date of the above Nov. 1" was & had been for some time staying with a loose woman passing her for his wife.

Sunday, November 12, 1865

Reuben Mauck of Co. "D" was brough[t] out from the city Early this Morning severely & dangerously stabed in the left Breast. was in a coffee House last eve. about 7 OK. with com[ra]d[e] & ladies eating supper[.] citizen wanted to Kill a Yank, & accordingly attempted Assassination.

Monday 13

Capt. .... of 58" Ills. Infty. was Robed last night of $300.00 [,] Watch [,] Revolvers etc.[99] Big Show begins two of them

98 The three jailed troopers were probably Privates Fielling and John Sexton, both young Missourians who had fought through most of the war, and Private John Barnes, who had already deserted twice in less than two years of army service. Thomas Hobson (or Hopson) was a veteran of four years in the service.

99 The 58th Illinois Volunteer Infantry Regiment, organized early in 1862, was destroyed as an effective fighting unit at Shiloh. Surviving remnants of this and other battered regiments temporarily formed the Union Brigade, Army of the Tennessee. The rebuilt 58th later saw much action in the west. It climaxed its combat career with the capture of Mobile, fighting with the 21st Missouri in the final assault on Fort Blakely. The 58th Illinois lost 83 men killed in action and another 215 dead of disease. It remained on occupation duty in Alabama until mustered out in April, 1866.

United circus & United States circus circus. and Seth Howes
great Europian circus & Menagerie beg[inn]ing on the 20"
Monday next. lively times in Mobile.[100]

Tuesday 14

went to the city & saw the Lady walk suspension Wire at Dr.
Harcus Show.[101] walked it up & down a distance of 200 feet.
went to the show in the Evening accompanied by a Lady friend
from Pascagoula not Miss. Cassimere my spanish Maiden, had
a real nice time. I could not enjoy it, thought I was in the
[w]rong pew.

Wednesday, November 15, 1865

went to the city to Market. played a game of Ball. Made out
dec. List for C.B. Lewis who is sick at Davenport Ia. went to
the city in the Evening & spent a few hours at my friends, which
by the way is a verry agreeable place to wile away leasure time.
I would be lost without some one [to] chit-chat with.

100 The United Circus began a week's engagement in Mobile on Monday,
November 13, giving two performances a day and charging a dollar for
admission. Coming from a successful stand in New Orleans and stressing
horses, acrobats, and clowns, it was the first circus Mobile had seen in many
weary years. Thayer and Noyes' U. S. Circus, a similar outfit, arrived from
Montgomery on November 14 for a one-week stand. The following week,
S. B. Howes' Great European Circus arrived and presented similar enter-
tainment for two more weeks. The enthusiastic people of Mobile filled the
tents for every performance of these circuses.

101 Every afternoon prior to the normal performance, the United Circus
presented "The Great Free Exhibition," i.e., a wire ascension outside the
regular tent.

Thursday 16

forwarded Dec. List of C.B.L. The two Horses that were stolen
were discovered by 1 of 119 Ills. (who is dis[charged] & stoping
in Mobile) out near spring-hill & restored to Lt.[102] S.A.R.B.-
P.M.[103] no trace of the Thief as yet. The Man Mauck who was
stabed is recovering.[104]

Friday 17

The whole Q. M. Dept. is out to day for a race did not go out
to see it have not heard how it came out. Bostwick & others
gets drunk makes more nois[e] than so many young Bulls in a
rage. I am reading a Book Entitled "Following the Flag" by
Carleton, for past time. Verry interesting.[105]

Saturday, November 18, 1865

nothing of interest transpired during the day. recd. compli-

[102] The 119th Illinois Volunteer Infantry Regiment was organized in
October, 1862 but saw little action until the last year of the war. Its combat fatalities totaled only 24 men, but it lost another 133 to disease. The
regiment participated in the seige of Mobile, including the assault on
Fort Blakely, and then remained on occupation duty in Mobile until mustered out on August 26, 1865. Spring Hill, home of Spring Hill College, was
a few miles to the northwest of Mobile.

[103] "S.A.R.B.P.M." probably means "Stolen Articles Returned By Provost
Marshal."

[104] Although seriously injured, Private Reuben Mauck not only recovered
but lived through the rest of the nineteenth century. He finally died in
Pleasant Grove, Nebraska, in January, 1901. See entry for November 12 for
description of his stabbing.

[105] *Following the Flag. From August, 1861, to Nov., 1862, with the Army
of the Potomac* by "Carleton" (Boston: Ticknor & Fields, 1864, $1.50) was a
popular book at this time.

mentary ticket & went to the circus in the. Enjoyed the Evening quite well. There were some verry amuseing and En-
tertaining feats. Just as I left the canvas, learned there was a
man (Reb) Murdered inside by Reg. Solds.

Sunday 19

Wilsey bets 5 dollars that he can make a dorg Eat Mustard,
dorg wouldent Eat it, W. is sold.[106] Irishman says he can
whip any yank S – – – th in the 21"[.] Jones prompted by
Whiskey give a pr. of No. 10 size govts. in the mouth & he
hallowes Bloody Murther, takes it back.[107]

Monday 20

draw & issue clothing. go to Mustering Office & get Rools to
Muster out Det. of Drafted Men. go to the new circus (S.B.
Howes.) the best riding I Ever saw. Regs. & Negro Soldiers get
in a fight. 9 of Nigs are sent to Hospl. 4 not Expected to live.
Effects of cuts from Knives.[108]

Tuesday, November 21, 1865

Made out complete set of Muster out rolls for Drafted Men, in-

106 Unidentifiable, possibly a nickname.
107 Private Charles Jones was a tough veteran of many campaigns.
108 The image-conscious local press did not publicize every act of violence
and bloodshed that occurred in the area, and neither did it go out of its
way to antagonize the occupation forces. The *Mobile Daily Advertiser and
Register* did not mention this fracas. Mobile was plagued by numerous
murders in this period, and a Negro was very often the victim. (See entries
for November 21 and 22.)

cludeing Dec. for Each Man & Discharge. went to the New circus last night with capt. tis a good show. A Negroe insulted sentinel who shot him dead on the spot.[109]

Wednesday 22

went to the Mustering Office got the Men mustered out but could get no pay as the rolls was dated 23rd. 3 Negroes were killed at R.R. Depot. went to the city Eat Lager Beer & drank Oysters while my pard took his Lady to the show.

Thursday 23

went to the Paymasters got the boys paid off in full[.] Eat some more Beer. went to see & hear the "Rolande" Brothers & troop perform at Mobile Theatre.[110] most amuseing thing I ever saw, besides verry daring feats & Witty Jokes etc. etc.

Friday, November 24, 1865

wrote Triplicate copies of proceedings of Bd. of survey con-

[109] This probably refers to an incident the previous Saturday night. An army sentinel at a nearby camp ordered Nat, a freedman, to halt. When Nat tried to run away, the soldier shot him down. Since Negro life was cheap at this time, Woodruff may have been describing another similar incident.

[110] The Mobile Theatre was located on the southeast corner of Royal and Conti Streets, near the waterfront. Originally opened in 1855, it was presenting plays again two weeks after Federal troops occupied the city, charging as much as ten dollars for the best seats and as little as fifty cents a seat in the gallery and Negro sections. William and Henry Rollande, gymnasts, were only a part of "The Grand Combination Company from the Academy of Music, New Orleans," which presented a variety show nightly for a little over a week. Specializing in songs, dances, acrobatics, pantomine, and Negro dialect skits, this troupe drew large, enthusiastic audiences.

vened at subsistence Depot. (Hitchcocks Press.) in compliance
with S.O. No. 74, dated Hd. Qrs. Dist. of Mobile, Mobile Ala.
Nov. 21/65.[111] recd. complimentary Ticket & went to the circus. An other Race. T.H. rode 1 horse, did not go to see it.[112]

Saturday 25

A. Lettour, Wm. E. Robertson, L. Tyler, B.H. Whitely, B. B.
Wort & J. C. Wilson Pvts. Drafted Men who was Mustered out
on the 23d started home to day.[113] God speed them on their
hapy Erand of care & comfort for the loved ones at home. recd.
an other complimentary Ticket & went to the show.

Sunday 26

being a fine day. (altho twas uncomonly warm for this season
of the yr.) & haveing nothing else to do I took a stroll in the
city to see the fashionables & stand on the corners & watch
the ladies, & admire their muscular developments as they trip
round the corners & raise their skirts just to show their *ankles*
of course.

[111] Judge Henry Hitchcock, Alabama's first millionaire, was the first
man to publish a book in the state in 1822, but his main efforts were in the
cotton trade. He owned warehouses and other commercial property and
several large cotton compresses. "Hitchcock's Press" refers to one of these
steam-powered cotton compresses, of course, and not to a printing press. It
was located on Royal Street and officially designated by the army as Post and
Depot Commissary Office. In command was Captain Walter C. Arthur. (See
entry for November 9.)

[112] "T.H." was Woodruff's good friend Lieutenant Thomas H. Roseberry
who had recently been commissioned after only a few months as sergeant
major. (See entry for July 17 and note 19.)

[113] Privates Antwine (army spelling!) Lettour, William E. Robertson,
Levi Tyler, Burr H. Whitely, Barry B. Wort, and John C. Wilson were
drafted in November, 1864 for one-year terms of service.

Monday, November 27, 1865

Thomas C. Brookaw Pvt. of Co. "H" died last night at Marine Hospl. in this city, was buried to day at 2 oclock P.M.[114] This has been a solemn day for those in camp who Knows & feels the loss of a Brother Soldier, following the remains of a true & faithful comrad[e] to the Grave is the Solemnest part of a soldiers duty.

Tuesday 28

had a Regtl. Inspection by the Adjt. went to the city on a regular Bum. got about 7 sheets in the wind and then went to the circus to see Dan. Rice Manouver his Trick Mules. Dan has the reputation of being the greatest Jester of the day, & I think he deserves it.[115]

Wednesday 29

make out Estimate of C. C. and G. E. for month of Dec. &

114 The large U.S. Marine Hospital, built in 1842, was on St. Anthony Street between Bayou and Jefferson Streets. The nearby City Hospital, built in 1825, and the Providence Infirmary were the city's other major medical facilities.

115 Dan Rice and his trained horses and mules joined S. B. Howes' Circus during its last week in Mobile. Rice was a well-known river performer in this period. He usually transported his show by boat and performed in a tent on the riverside. Rice's career began long before the war. First a horse trainer, then a wrestler for P. T. Barnum, then a circus clown, he soon started his own show which featured pigs, mules, and horses. In the 1850's he toured with his own circus on the steamboat *Allegheny Mail.* As soon as the war ended, Rice resumed his riverside show business, and by 1869 his circus was famous and prosperous. The Panic of 1873 wrecked his circus, and his later efforts to make a comeback were unsuccessful. The old performer finally died in 1900. He should not be confused with Thomas Darmouth "Daddy" Rice, the creator of "Jim Crow" and the minstrel show, who died in 1860.

Dec. List of Deserters[.] this is Easily done as we have none the
last month. A mans hat is found in the suburbs of the city
with 2 Bullet holes in it & covered with Blood. looks suspicious
but no search made.

Thursday, November 30, 1865

went to the city strolled in to a Daguerrians & while gazeing
on the paintings presented to view 2 lady acquaintances steped
in, asked me to pay for an ambrotype of themselves.[116] I was
sold, could not get out of it. after it was completed, they presented it to me. Complimentary Indeed.

Friday, December 1

settled Mess accts. to 1" of Dec. made out schedule of C. C.
& G. E. for Nov. contemplated writing a letter to Carrie have
written two & feel tired. Knowing she will Excuse till tomorrow
I will postpone it. went to the circus last night feel sleepy.
Poor Excuse, but I pass.

Saturday 2

recd. Orders to report Lt. R.R.H. absent without leave, who
by the way is absent sick. went to the Theatre saw one of Rol-

---

[116] The best-known type of photograph at this time was the daguerreo-
type which was produced on a silver plate or a copper plate covered with
silver. The related ambrotype was a picture taken on a plate of prepared
glass in which the lights are represented in silver and the shades are produced by a dark background visible through the unsilvered portions of the
glass.

lande Bros. turn a summersault on stilts, a verry difficult feat, the only man I ever heard of doing it. lively times in the city, near Election day.

Sunday, December 3, 1865

Evrry body Electioneering for their candidates a Greater Excitement prevails than I ever Knew over a Presidential Election, some of our soldiers have been offered $25. to vote, others suits of clothing & so on. if you want a drink of Whiskey halloo for Moulton the Irishmans candidate.[117]

Monday 4

Soldiers are ordered to stay in camp, dont do it. Bill Massey, I. Longcor & Mauck gets in a mess.[118] Massey gets cut in two places in left arm, Longcor in the breast, all slight. Jim Roseberry comes to camp drunk, says he voted 6 times & got fifty dollars for it, a good days work.

Tuesday 5

Sam Davalt & Corporal Joseph Sherrick returns from furlough.

[117] This city election was held on Monday, December 4. A mayor was chosen. One councilman and three alderman from each of the city's seven wards were also elected at this time. In the main contest for mayor, C. F. Moulton was narrowly defeated by Jones Mitchell Withers, a former mayor and, more important, a former Confederate general. The local newspapers provided only limited coverage of this contest and pictured it as a rather routine affair.

[118] On this occasion the ever-unreliable Privates Isaac Longcor and Mathew Mauck were joined by Private William F. Massey, who had fought in three major battles in his year of wartime service and was still only 19 years old.

Anderson has not been heard from. my Pascagoula friend
mooves into or near a place Known in camp by a verry hard
name as well as Illfame. begin to loose confidence. One I know
will proove true, my absent Carrie.

Wednesday, December 6, 1865

Anderson is reported absent without leave. I. Longcor & M.
Mauck have not been heard from since Early yesterday Morning[,] report them to day as Deserters. make application for a
Furlough for Rees H. Roseberry & Theodore Harrison. Capt.
is verry sick Effects of continued drunkeness.

Thursday 7

Murch furlough was disapprooved at Regtl. Hd. Qrs. Rs & Hs
come back for correction in Endorsement, have modified the
Regulations since the last I went to Dept. Hd. Qrs. prefered
charges and specifications against Jno. W. Masterson for ne-
glect of duty while on guard.[119]   * see Note 5. Jan. 31"

Note 5. refered from 7" December

Greathouse[,]Holcomb & Nate Longcor go the city on a Bum
comeing back pas some regulars on the cor[ner] (10) in number & begin singing "I'll never jump the bounty any more"

[119] Private John W. Masterson was a tall, dark veteran of four years of
combat who still liked a good fight. (See entry for December 14.)

regs take it as an insult & make fight.[120] Are geting the better
of them & about to use them up when speckled Dick "Mounted
Orderly" comes along & instead of stoping to help them out,
put spurs to his horse & gave the alarm in the camp, Co. "G"
reinforces & drives regs to camp, regs reinforce & drive them
back. Things looks rather squally & this juncture believe there
will be a general Riot. We have some faithful Negroe cooks who
Join in the fray. "G" reinforces again when the Maj. & off. of
the day interfere & order a cesation of hostilities. Regular off.
sends out Guards & takes his men back to camp. Thus it ends
for the present. none of our men are seriously hurt. G, H & L.
are all prety badly banged about the Nose & face but not dangerous. Dr. Roberts servant gov. was badly bruised on the head
& arm quite broken. The 15" (that is the regulars) have to
carry several of their men to camp. Clubs brickbats & Knives
were freely used. Many will carry their marks to the grave, &
some, I predict will go there soon & from this cause. There is
quite a hatred existing between the two Regiments which will
never be overcome as long as they remain in such close proxim-
ity. Tis dangerous for either party to meet one of the oposite
alone after night, & I might correctly say in daylight. I might
assign a reason for this hatred but I will defer it untill some
other time. We may hear from them again soon. 1" Sergt. Baker
Co. "C" & Sergt. Matlick Co. "D" go to the city, get intoxicated
& come back quite excited.[121] Baker has a severe wound in
right arm, & Matlick bruised up in the face. Say they got in a

120 The three brawlers from Company G were Privates John Greathouse
and George N. Longcor, both young veterans of four years of combat, and
Private William H. Holcomb, who had enlisted early in 1864 and participated
in several bloody engagements before the war ended. Still full of fight, they
found the regulars of the 15th U.S. Infantry Regiment convenient substitutes for rebels.

121 Sergeant W. H. Matlick quickly recovered and lived to see the dawn of
the twentieth century. His more seriously injured comrade, Sergeant Baker,
is not positively identifiable.

fight & Baker was shot. some one who was near at the time says
his curiosity was excited by some Jewelry in a stand & in the act
of attempting to abstract some of the sparkling Gems cut his
arm on the Glass. Did not wait to have the case opened for
his convenience, forced his hand through the Glass, thus paying for his adventure by spilling his own blood. Good Experience for a man providing he does not shed too mutch of it.

Friday 8

All is Quiet today, quite a heavy white frost here this morning.
Capt. gets his new Milty. clothing from Keokuk. promises to
make me a present of a suit. Get the Presidents Message, re-
mooves the gloom of many hearts, all pleased with it.[122]

Saturday, December 9, 1865

went to the Commissary & laid in a supply of rations for the
Mess. went to the city met an old acquaintance from Pascagoula Keeping an Oyster saloon in the Evening[.] went to a

[122] After hailing Lincoln, the Union, and the United States Constitution,
President Andrew Johnson optimistically described his efforts—"almost
imperceptable steps"—to restore the vitality of the southern states and then
championed the Thirteenth Amendment as the final restorer of national
harmony. He said that it remained only for the southern states to return
representatives to Congress, but added that Congress could judge the qualifi-
cations of its own members. This speech offered something to every faction
and was generally moderate. Woodruff and his comrades were pleased, not
because the President offered the South an easy road back into the Union,
but because his policy seemed to promise rapid demobilization and an easy
road home for weary troopers.

dance out near spring Hill about 3 miles from this city North.[123]

Sunday 10

did not get back from the party till a late hour & being some-what tired out danceing & walking from there to camp & the Elements appearing somewhat blustery I concluded I could im-proove the time about as well in bed as anywhere else, slept all day.

Monday 11

in makeing the detail this morning I discovered we had lost an other man by Desertion[.] Pvt. Jacob Glessner took his Musket with him[,] suppose he intends to fight his way through. Jno. W. Masterson appears before the court for trial.

Tuesday, December 12, 1865

Get an Order detailing Pvt. M. Bishop for duty at Dept. Head Quarters. make out Invoices & receipts for camp & garrison Equipage turned over. The boys are begining to fish again, have good luck. Butcher caught a nice one to day is as proud of it as a plantation Negroe of a brass Ear ring.

[123] During the war a narrow-guage railroad was built from Mobile to Spring Hill, but Woodruff easily walked there from his camp on the western outskirts of Mobile.

Wednesday 13

has been raining for three successive days looks like clearing off this morning but is verry cold & disagreeable. ruffer weather than I Ever Expected to see in the sunny sunny south as its called. forward Requisitions for Fuel.

Thursday 14

still boisterous & cold with a severe wind almost a gale from the North. considerable frost this morning with some Ice. I pass my time in Keeping fires in my little camp stove & reading one of Mrs. Gores Novels, Entitled Too Old A Bird too be caught with chaff.[124]   * see Note 6. Feb. 10".

Note 6 refered from December. 14"

While quietly reading to myself in my little soldier abode, I was startled by cries of rally, rally, fallin 21" they are chargeing us, which at once awakened within me a sence of danger, & brought to memory thrilling recollections of past scenes where Bloody but noble deeds have been transacted. On Emerging from my tent I discovered Joe Wright, Corpl Matticker of Co. "F" & others[125] comeing up street with a dozen or two of the 15" U.S. close after them with Bayonets, & looking through the camp men & Officers were running too & fro & some were under arms & loading their pieces as if prepareing for action. The col. comeing up halted the squad from the 15" & asked the cause of

[124] *Too Old a Bird to be Caught with Chaff* (New York: F.A. Brady, 1865, 50¢) was written by Catherine Grace Frances (Moody) Gore, a prolific novelist.
[125] Private Joseph S. Wright was a veteran. Corporal Matticker is unidentifiable.

alarm, whereupon all setup a jabering, & all I could learn was
that—somebody was hurt & Joe was the offender. The col. there-
fore delivered him over to the squad who pretended to be
Guards with authority, & they marched him off out of site our
camp & there fell upon him nearly beating him to death & then
sent him back to camp, he is now in hospitle. Our men are in-
dignant sware they wont stand it. While this is going on, Geo.
Wagoner of Co. "F" who is on detail at Dept. Hdqrs. is comeing to camp & passes a saloon where some of his own Co. are
drinking. They see him & pounce on him saying we will make
you remember so & so. An old grudge, (he was, if not now a
Non Comd. Off.) & beat him in a shocking manner, he goes
back to Hdqrs. & reports the facts. Maj. Grosskopff Asst. Insptr.
Genl. mounts his horse & rides out to our camp to investigate the
case, meanwhile Genl. De Russy hearing of it sends the col a
note to investigate it & if possible bring the offender to justice,
while this is going on.[126] Masterson concludes he must have a
mess of Regulars & accordingly him, Greathouse[,]Corpl. Massey of Co. "G" [127] & others set off down the street & in about
15 minutes we hear the cry of rally, 21" turn out & help us we
are being overpowered etc. Several men arm themselves with
Bricks, clubs, Knives or anything they can get hold of, & proceed
to the field at once. Col. Best appears, orders the Regt. under
Arms, Capt. Shafer Co. "E" to take command,[128] while he runs

[126] Brigadier General Gustavus Adolphus De Russy was an effective artillery officer in the eastern theater of operations during the war. He was
briefly assigned to the Department of Alabama at the end of the war. Major Edward Grosskopff, a native of Ohio, served throughout the war as an
artillery officer.
[127] Corporal Frank A. Massey's previous difficulties are mentioned in the
entries for July 20 and 25 and August 23. Privates John W. Masterson and
John Greathouse were in trouble as recently as December 7.
[128] The young commander of the regiment, Colonel Joseph G. Best, has
been identified previously. Captain Emanuel B. Shafer, a native of Ohio,
was another youthful officer with much combat experience.

off down the street to try & settle the riot, the Regt. about 90
in all are in readiness in a moment. look down the street & we
[see] 8 or 10 of our men on the retreat one man firing a revolver
& the rest manfully contesting the ground with bricks against
a hundred or more of the 15" who darken the air with their
bricks & other Missiles. Maj. Grosskopff has been playing check-
ers mounts his horse & rides to the camp of the 15" gets a
mounted officer & returns to the field. Capt. S. brings up his
men on double quick & at the sight of Bayonets the, the victory
is changed to a defeat & the 15" flee for their camp, closely followed by the 21". The Orders are not to fire, so when they are
safely within their camp Capt. S. thinking there is no farther
kneed of an escort orders a change of front to the rear & we
return to camp. This is my first appearance under arms since
I recd. my wound at fort Blakely Apl. 9"/65. & as luck would
have it I did not get under fire this time. Masterson was dangerously if not fatally injured by haveing his face brutally mangled
& skull fractured, he is now in Hospital. Surgeon thinks the
chances are as largely against him as for him. Think if he has
not got a mess this time, he had beter try again. I think however
he will be a little reluctant & call at some other firm for the
next mess. I was informed this Evening Dec. 15" that three of
the 15" had died of the Effects of the riot. I heard the dead-
march played once to day in their camp. There was an other
Excitement to day but it is geting so late I will retire for the
night & tell you of it tomorrow or some other day when Ive
nothing else to do. My nerves are somewhat unsteady from the
Excitement of the day but nevertheless I believe I can sleep
soundly & dream of loved ones far away; Au Revoir.

Friday, December 15, 1865

This Morning when I arose I found Ice in a cup I had left

standing on my Table half full of Water, it was frozen sollid. notwithstanding I Kept fire in my stove untill a late hour last night. Matters look quite hostile, great Excitement.   * see Note 7 Feb. 27.

Note 7. refered from Dec. 15"

Well as I said in my Memoranda "Great Excitement" so it was for those days when there is no Wars, or rumors of Wars. but to my story, in my last Note I believe I was telling you of roits, conquests & so on, now I will tell you of a strong Mutiny which is One of the verry strongest Open Violation of Military Law and Discipline. I have been waiting till this late day to record the case (this is the 20" of Dec.) in Order if possible to get the correct details, and from the information I can gather the facts are about as follows, Viz. Maj. McGonigle, Capt. Shafer, M.N. Sinnott & Ike Johnson of 21" Mo.[129] went to a grocery on New Market St. only one sqr. from here to get them a cigar, while at the Bar they heard the sound of revelry in a back-room to which they paid no attention but just as they emerged from the door to return to the camp, some half Doz. men burst from the room, all N.C.O. but One, and all from the 15th U.S.I. and began abuseing Our Officers. The Pvt. of the squad told the Maj. he would whip him & followed him towards camp, telling the "damned Bloody Hoosiers, to hunt their holes." The Maj. procured a Gard and went back to arrest the perpetrator or slanderer. The revelers upon seeing the Guard ran in back rooms hideing in dry-goods Boxes, & even into the Ladies Bedroom under the beds. The Guards went in & brought out the hole squad, I sergt. swore he would not be taken Prisoner,

[129] Major Henry McGonigle, Captain Emanuel B. Shafer, and First Lieutenant Martin N. Sinnott have been mentioned previously. Sergeant Jonathan Johnson was in Company H.

all the damned hoosiers in the city could not take him. Capt.
Shafer a verry bold and dareing fellow by the way, drew his
revolver, cocked it & presented it to his ear and politely informed him that he could take him whereupon the man surrendered by cooly asking the capt. "how long since he left the
Highway." The Maj. pointed out the would be "Assassin" &
the rest were informed if they could go to their Quarters & be-
have like soldiers in the future they was at liberty to do so.
brought the prisoner whom I shall call *Charley Howard* to the
camp, wrote out charges and specifications against him and sent
a large escort of Bayonets to conduct him to the Provost Mar-
tials who put him in what we call a cross bared hotel showed
him a snug little room & turned a Key on him that he was not
a[t] liberty to Carry. he is now in Irons, verry comfortable tobe-
sure, although I presume he would today prefer the "Monotonies of a camp life." While this was going on, the revelers was
not idle, even before the escort had returned, they could be
seene congregateing in large numbers on the same corner where
the arrest was made, and under Orders, they formed in line of
Battle, loaded their pieces, fixed Bayonets & advanced on our
camp when at the Edge of the camp the halt, Order Arms,
and the Sergt. in comd. (I have not learned his name.) sends
an Orderly to the col's tent with a dispatch the nature of which
I did not learn, the col. who knows nothing of what is going on
outside yet, receives the dispatch, & the Orderly returns to his
comrads. Col. Best Opens the dockument and comes out and
joins a Squad of Our Offs. who have congregated there to see
what the display is all about. The sergt. in comd. counts off a
detail of six men assigns a corpl. to comd. & they advance in
to the camp, they look round & see comeing across an open
lot, on double quick, the Officer of the day in the 15th. They
waver and stop. The cries from the main column to go on,
go on, bring him Out etc. arrouse the men of our camp, and

many, not (verry many either for we have only about 30 men
in camp.) come and look on the scene, and a sensation causes
them to believe they will soon be called to *Action,* and those
noble soldiers who have stood where Missiles of death flew like
frozen hale & as thick & fast, and have walked unflinchingly
up to the long lines of flame & glitering steel on many a bloody
field, said not a word, but returned in silence to their Tents,
buckled on their Armor loaded their arms and quietly awaited
for the cry to "fallin, fallin." The Mutineers advance & halt
again. Col. Joe. goes out to see what it means, and by this time
the reg. Off. comes up and deliberately Orders them back to
camp. They refuse to go. he inquires what they want, they say
they want Charley Howard. Col. Joe. says you cant have him,
we will have him or we'll have blood, we'll clean out you d—d
hoosiers, the Off. asks the name & Co. of the comdr. & orders
them back again. They shoulder arms, left face, come to a front
and refuse to go till col. Joe, releases the prisoner and gives
him up to them. Col. Joe. says if I call out my men, you will
go back. Again they are Ordered & persuaded. The[y] all cheer
& say reenforcements are comeing we will have him yet. A
squad comes down the road on the double quick & joins them.
The Officers after a good deal more parleying and Ordering
get them started to camp. They go off cheering & hallowing
to give up Charley Howard you bloody cusses etc. etc. Our
men unbuckle their armor verry thankful they are spared the
pain of sheding a Brother Soldiers Blood. They do not deserve
to be called Brother Soldiers, but still we are bound to respect
them as such. The Maj. & other Officers of the 15" come down
who appear verry mutch surprised when they are informed of
the conduct of their men, on this occasion as well as the others
I have spoken of, and say they knew nothing of it hereto-
fore. They go round in our hospl. & inspect our wounded (of
which I have spoken before) & get all the information they

can gather on the subject and return to camp with a full de-
termination to punish the gilty. I believe they are sincere in
what they say, & will visit the revelers with their just retribu-
tion, a verry Gentlemanly set of Officers appearantly. Genl. De
Russy sends out a staff Off. to investigate the case. We learn
they have a plan concocted to charge our camp tonight. (or
at least that night.) which was the 15" of Dec. but ere night
is upon us we are informed that they are all in arrest & confined under a strong guard, so we go to rest on our little comely
couches & sleep soundly till the morn without disturbance. The
five N.C.O., 4 of their 1st Sergts and 1 duty sergt, who were
at the Saloon at the time of the arrest, went to their camp &
Ordered their companies into line to rescue the prisoner, this
was the force that came to our camp between 3 & 4 hundred
strong. Quite enough to have swallowed our little band of 30
men bayonets & all at one gulf, but we did not think so, couldent
see it. if they had of been the right kind of men they would
have whiped us verry easily. Suppose they would anyhow if
we had fought, but the little volunteer band could not think
of yielding without a strugle. "They have danced to the music
before and on many a broad and spacious field." The five Ser-
geants are now in military prison with others awaiting in Irons
their trial which commences tomorrow. The charges against
them are verry severe, and the probabilaty is that they will
be shot, not only as a punishment for their own crimes, but
as a warning to others, as an Example to the Army, which if
such be the case, I hope all will heed in the future. I was
slightly acquainted with some of them, 1st Sergt. Russell & duty
sergt. Tulley, in fact I have been introduced to all of them
prior to the unfortunate day I speak of, but I disremember their
names, & so far as my Knowledge goes they were likely young
Men with fair prospects in life, & I must say they all treated me
verry Gentlemanly and with respect. I cannot help but feel

sorry that their prospects are so soon blighted & their own hands, or perhaps love for some dear friend, connected with the curse of intoxication[,] furnished the barrier, and thus they are cut off in the bloom of life, in the vigor of Manhood. I am going down to see them the first opportunity, then perhaps I can tell you more about it, till then adieu.

Saturday 16

The morning is beautiful & fair, but before night the weather has changed to the mild Winter of the North & it is raining a cold rain again. no riots to day no body drunk all is quiet on the Ala. Prepare some official documents for the captain.

Sunday 17

This is a calm beautiful morning. The capt. is verry sick. forward some Official papers. General De Russy comes Out & inspects the camp. 1" Lt. Allen of Co. "G" now Actg. Asst. Provost Martial comes out to see us. Take a walk in the city, the only means I have to wile away the lonesome hours.

Monday, December 18, 1865

Awake to find the city and surrounding country Enveloped in a dense Fog so thick you can almost Knock it into showers of rain by strikeing it with a club. The water falls from the trees like it does after a heavy shower as the fog drifts along.

Tuesday 19

The fog continues. occasional glimps[e] of sunshine but the
dazling Orb soon disappears again & the fog drifts on. The
captains Ord. returns for 3d Qr. of 64 as O.O. 3d Div. is returned for correction.[130] go to the city & get a Barrel of Oysters
in the shell have a fine supper.

Wednesday 20

make out and forward Dec. List of S. Snyder. Our wounded
rioters are geting along finely, much better than Expected. M.
who was burnt with powder has quite recovered. on my usual
round to the Market I was much amused at Nig. sentinel takeing a "Jack Tar" to the "Lock up"

Thursday, December 21, 1865

Make out Dec. List for M. Bishop. The furloughs for Roseberry & Harrison come back to Co. approoved. R. is going over
to Fort Blakely tomorrow to disinter the remains of his Brother
Killed there in Apl. I am going with him. They will start for
home saturday.

Friday 22

Embarked at 10 Ock A.M. on Stmr. "Senator" in Co. with R.H.

---

130 Captain Edward K. Blackburn's performance as divisional ordnance
officer was evidently not flawless.

Roseberry & five men. arrive at Fort Blakeley 1 Ock P.M.[131]
went to the Burial Ground disintered the remains of Sergt. Matthias Roseberry who was Killed at the above named place Apl.
9" 1865. reembarked at 11½ Ock in Eve.

Saturday 23

Arrived at Mobile at 4 Ock this morning with the remains
which is badly decomposed. R. H. R. & T.H.R. & T. H. start
north with the remains at 4 Oclock P.M. have a furlough for
Thirty days. weather is quite cold so mutch the better for their
sorrowfull mission.

Sunday, December 24, 1865

Just prepareing to write to Carrie when lo an Orderly rides
up, the "Pack up call" Beats, & at 4 Ock we are on the march!
Embark on Bd. Tug Rolla & a flat which she tows & start up
the Ala. River at 7 oclock in Eve. spoils our Christmas was
going to spring hill.

Monday 25

The Fog was so thick had to lay up till morn. landed at the
Mt. Vernon arsenal at daylight. march out to the arsenal 3

---

[131] The *Senator* was formerly a Confederate vessel based at Mobile. Just
before the battle of Mobile Bay, it had helped tow the doomed ram *Tennessee* off of a sandbar and back into deep water.

miles from river.[132] Co. of Nigs. here, beautiful place. Boys all get drunk that are in habit of drinking, merry time. Nigs have a Grand Ball. cant mix.

Tuesday 26

Go to work early fix up desks & so on to get ready for the rush of business just now comeing out. poor Quarters, looks like soldiering again. some lady liveing in arsenal comes down with complaint that some of our men have stolen her calf. saw fresh meat, could not help her.

Wednesday, December 27, 1865

S. D. Mail Messenger departed for Mobile. Greathouse & Davis are missing supposed to have Deserted. Lt. Harris returns & joins Co. for duty. went out hunting round the woods all day did not catch a clam. capt. shot a squirrel. got an invitation to dinner on sunday next, & to drink an egg-nog for Newyears.

Thursday 28

A detail goes to Mobile for our Tents. The Capt. & Wilsey goes Guning after hunting all day get nothing but 3 chickens

132 Mount Vernon, 27 miles to the north of Mobile, was established in 1811 as a military post, and in the late 1820's it became an arsenal. When Alabama seceded, state troops seized this vital installation. It remained an arsenal until 1895 when the Federal government gave it to the state. Finally it became part of the state hospital for Negro insane. Technically, Mount Vernon is near the Mobile River a few miles south of the confluence of the Alabama and Tombigbee Rivers, Mobile's water routes into the interior of the state.

& a squirrel. Lewis and Longcor are out & get lost in the swamp, employ a guide to bring them out. spend the day writing on Muster Rolls, the weather is beautiful.

Friday 29

Make out anual Return of causalities for the year of 1865. Capt. & Wilsey goes hunting catch nothing. go fishing get some nice cats & an Ell. Lt. Ambrose Joins command.[133] Make a bunk for accomodation of 2, expect to moove soon again, as soon as we get fixed comfortable.

Saturday, December 30, 1865

Capt. & Wilsey goes guning with 1 days rations & 2 canteens of Licker, they expect a merry time. I expect they'll have a hell of a drunk. complet[e] annual return, monthly return, descriptive List of deserters, & Quarterly return of deceased soldiers. Tents arrive from Mobile.

Sunday 31

The Hunters return just at night wet through & through. been raining all day which of course wet the out side, and they wet the other with poison Whiskey as their appearance Indicate, however they bring in a Ham of Venison, luckier than usual. have a lot of official documents finished & ready to forward[.] the capt. is too drunk to sign them. Mustered for Pay. There is now six months pay due us, I have my Muster Rolls ready

133 Possibly Mordecai J. W. Ambrose.

to forward tomorrow morning. This is the last day of the year
1865, & still finds me a Soldier, five Christmas days I've spent
in the Army.   * see Note 8 30" March.

Note 8 refered from Dec. 31" 1865

last night Private Jones of A Co.[134] being on Guard got drunk
(nothing strange however for him, for I dont know of him
drawing a sober breath since my return to the company on the
10" day of last July.) & mad[e] an effort to shoot a Man by
the name of *Becker* Superintendent of some works in the Arsenal here, by snaping 2 caps at him his Gun missing fire, got
mad & broke it over a tree, swareing he had Quit Soldiering,
was arrested & tied too a post about half an hour, after a faithful promise to go to bed & keep still & preserve the peace he
was let down, but no sooner down, than he takes out his Knife
threatens evry one he doesent like, & declares he will Kill the
man that ordered him tied up. he is tied again with Orders too
Keep him there till morning, being now about 9 oclock. tied
him to a limb of a tree by the camp fire, remains about an
hour and a half, pulls loose & runs away from the guard, sleeps
in the woods till the morning, rains all night, comes in in the
morning looking as though he had lost his last friend, is arrested again and confined. Becker has prefered charges, have
not saw them, but presume they will be verry severe, the Maj.
is also going to prefer charges, and perhaps the Co Comdr.
Tis the first time he has ever been punished since he has been
in the Army nearly five years. has been a good soldier, but
would get drunk, it hurts my feelings to see men that have

[134] Private Edward Jones was another young veteran who was sick of
army life. After being mustered out, he settled down to a long, respectable
life in La Bell, Missouri.

staked their lives on a thousand Battle fields & prooved themselves men amongst men & the best men the world ever knew,
disgrace themselves now the war is over and just on the eve of
home and happiness, and for nothing, but such is nature I believe with some. I have often heard him say he was a ruined
Man, had become desperate, was lost, bound to go to hell any
how, and he'd be damned if he dident raise hell while he did
live, and many other sutch remarks. God have mercy on sutch
men for they have none for themselves or no one else, God
bless you till we meet again & a happy New Years *from your
friend Matt.*

So ends the diary. Sergeant Woodruff's military career ended
three months later on April 3, 1866, with a terse, official report
listing him as a deserter. The 21st Missouri was mustered out
honorably only sixteen days later, but Woodruff, like many other citizen-soldiers in the army of occupation, simply could wait
no longer. A fine combat trooper and a patriot, he was also a
restless, freedom-loving American who could no longer stomach
the dreary regimentation of army life. Thus Sergeant Mathew
Woodruff disappears into the mainstream of American life,
an apt symbol of his country's failure to win the peace. Both
Woodruff and his government, having won the war, lacked the
clear principles and steady patience to reconstruct the battered
Union "with liberty and justice for all." [135]

[135] Service and pension records of Mathew Woodruff, National Archives.
Woodruff went directly back home to Clark County, Missouri, married
Sarah Carrie Springer, and settled down to farm and raise a family. A few
years later he took his wife and two children to a farm in Kansas. By this
time a special act of Congress had erased his technical desertion from the
record, and he was receiving a disability pension for his wartime wound.
Later Woodruff and his family moved westward again to Lee County, Iowa.
Here he died on March 3, 1882, at the age of 39. He was survived by his
wife, a daughter, Jesse, and a son, Mark.

Select Bibliography

MANUSCRIPTS

The Diary of Sergeant Mathew Woodruff. Henry E. Huntington Library, San Marino, California.

The Regimental Book of the 21st Missouri Infantry, Records of the Adjutant General's Office, Record Group 94, National Archives (microfilm).

Compiled Service Records of Volunteer Union Soldiers Who Served in Organizations from the State of Missouri, Role 549, Twenty-first Infantry, National Archives (microfilm).

Descriptive Roll of Company G, 21st Regiment, and Service Record of Mathew Woodruff, Company G, 21st Regiment, Adjutant General's Office, State of Missouri, Jefferson City, Missouri.

NEWSPAPER

Mobile Daily Advertiser and Register, 1865-1866. Unfortunately, no newspaper from the Pascagoula area in the immediate postwar period has survived.

OFFICIAL AND CONTEMPORARY ACCOUNTS

Annual Report of the Adjutant General of Missouri for the Year Ending December 31, 1865. Jefferson City: Emory S. Foster, 1866.

Battles and Leaders of the Civil War. 4 vols. New York: The Century Company, 1884-1887.

The 21st Missouri Regiment Infantry Veteran Volunteer Association. Proceedings of Annual Re-Unions. 1888–1902. Fort Madison, Iowa: Roberts & Roberts, 1903.

The War of the Rebellion: A Compilation of the Official Records of the Union and Confederate Armies. 130 vols. Washington: Government Printing Office, 1880–1901.

THESIS

Isbell, Frances Annette. "A Social and Economic History of Mobile, 1865–1875." Unpublished Master's thesis, University of Alabama, 1951.

GENERAL BOOKS

Adams, George Worthington. *Doctors in Blue: The Medical History of the Union Army in the Civil War.* New York: Henry Schuman, 1952.

Boatner, Mark M., III. *The Civil War Dictionary*. New York: David McKay Company, 1959.

Black, Robert C., III. *The Railroads of the Confederacy*. Chapel Hill: The University of North Carolina Press, 1952.

Brooks, Stewart. *Civil War Medicine*. Springfield, Illinois: Charles C. Thomas, 1966.

Capers, Gerald M. *Occupied City: New Orleans Under the Federals: 1862–1865*. Frankfort: University of Kentucky Press, 1965.

Catton, Bruce. *This Hallowed Ground: The Story of the Union Side of the Civil War*. Garden City, New York: Doubleday & Company, 1956.

———. *The American Heritage Picture History of the Civil War*. New York: American Heritage Publishing Company, Inc., 1960.

Delaney, Caldwell. *The Story of Mobile*. Mobile: Gill Printing Co., 1953.

Dyer, Frederick H. *A Compendium of the War of the Rebellion*. 3 vols. New York: Thomas Yoseloff, 1959.

Fleming, Walter L. *Civil War and Reconstruction in Alabama*. Cleveland: The Arthur H. Clark Company, 1911.

Ficklen, John Rose. *History of Reconstruction in Louisiana (Through 1868)*. Baltimore: The Johns Hopkins Press, 1910.

Franklin, John Hope. *Reconstruction: After the Civil War*. Chicago: University of Chicago Press, 1961.

Garner, James Wilford. *Reconstruction in Mississippi*. New York: The Macmillan Company, 1901.

Headley, J. T. *Farragut and Our Naval Commanders*. New York: E. B. Treat & Co., 1867.

Heitman, Francis B. *Historical Register and Dictionary of the United States Army, From Its Organization, September 29, 1789, to March 2, 1903*. 2 vols. Urbana: University of Illinois Press, 1965.

Jones, Virgil Carrington. *The Civil War at Sea*. 3 vols. New York: Holt, Rinehart & Winston, 1960–1962.

Moses, Montrose J. *Famous Actor-Families in America*. New York: Thomas Y. Crowell & Company, 1906.

Powell, Colonel Wm. H. *List of Officers of the Army of the United States from 1779 to 1900: Embracing a Register of All Appointments by the President of the United States in the Volunteer Service During the Civil War and of Volunteer Officers in the Service of the United States June 1, 1900*. New York: L. R. Hamersly & Co., 1900.

Randall, J. G. and Donald, David. *The Civil War and Reconstruction*. Boston: D. C. Heath & Company, 1961.

Reid, Whitelaw. *After the War: A Tour of the Southern States: 1865–1866*. New York: Harper & Row, 1965.

Reinders, Robert C. *End of an Era: New Orleans, 1850–1860*. New Orleans: Pelican Publishing Company, 1964.

Sefton, James E. *The United States Army and Reconstruction: 1865–1877*. Baton Rouge: Louisiana State University Press, 1967.

Shannon, Fred Albert. *The Organization and Administration of the Union Army: 1861–1865*. 2 vols. Cleveland: The Arthur H. Clark Company, 1928.

Stampp, Kenneth M. *The Era of Reconstruction, 1865–1877*. New York: Alfred A. Knopf, 1965.

Taylor, George Rogers and Neu, Irene D. *The American Railroad Network: 1861–1890*. Cambridge, Massachusetts: Harvard University Press, 1956.

Warner, Ezra J. *Generals in Blue: Lives of the Union Commanders.* Baton Rouge: Louisiana State University Press, 1964.

Wiley, Bell Irvin. *The Life of Billy Yank: The Common Soldier of the Union.* New York: The Bobbs-Merrill Company, 1952.

Workers of the Writers' Program of the Work Projects Administration in the State of Alabama. *Alabama: A Guide to the Deep South.* New York: Hastings House, 1941.

Workers of the Writers' Program of the Work Projects Administration in the State of Louisiana. *Louisiana: A Guide to the State.* New York: Hastings House, 1941.

Workers of the Writers' Program of the Work Projects Administration in the State of Missouri, *Missouri: A Guide to the "Show Me" State.* New York: Duell, Sloan & Pearce, 1941.

Writers' Project of the Works Progress Administration. *Mississippi: A Guide to the Magnolia State.* New York: The Viking Press, 1938.

Index

N.B.—Most of the references in this Index are to date of entry in the diary rather than to page numbers in the book. When reference is made to page numbers, these appear first and in boldface type. References to footnotes, identified as such, are given last.

E.g.: PASCAGOULA, MISSISSIPPI, **8**; July 8–September 14; *footnote* 15.

Alice Vivian, July 6

Allen, Lt. Daniel R., October 10, December 17; *footnote* 66

Alvis brothers, Hiram J. and Edward H., August 13

Ambrose, Lt. Mordicai J. W., December 29

Antone, Capt., August 17

Anderson, Pvt. William, November 2, 6, December 5, 6

Arthur, Capt. Walter C., November 9, 11; *footnote* 95

Baker, Sgt., December 7

Ball game, November 7, 8, 9, 15

Barnes, Pvt. John, *footnote* 98

Bates, Pvt. Martin W., August 3, 16, 18; *footnote* 32

Bathing: *see* Swimming

Baton Rouge, Louisiana, July 5

Battle House, Mobile, November 5
Becker, Mr., December 31
Best, Col. Joseph G., October 23, 24,
    December 14, 31; footnote 80
Bishop, Pvt. Mordica, September
    27, October 31, November 6,
    December 12, 21; footnote 58
Blackburn, Capt. Edward K., July
    15, 16, 24, August 6–10, 19, 23,
    26, 28, 29, September 6, 15, 20,
    October 9–12, 16, 27,
    November 3, 4, 10, 21, December
    6, 8, 16, 17, 19, 27–31; footnotes
    17, 22, 29, 84, 130
Bonnie Blue Flag, October 17
Bostwick, Pvt. Henry S., October
    20, November 17
Brookaw, Pvt. Thomas C., November
    27
Burns, Lt. George H., October
    15; footnote 69
Butcher, Sgt. John W., July 17,
    August 1, 3, 5, 25, September
    23, 25, December 12; footnote
    19

Cairo, Illinois, June 30
"Carleton," November 17
Carr, Pvt. Richard, October 26;
    footnote 83
Cassimere, Miss, July 19, 21, 23,
    November 14
Chicago, October 17
Christmas, December 24
Church, Cpl. George S., September
    27, October 2, 31, November 6
Cincinnati, October 17
Circus, November 13, 14, 18, 20,
    21, 24, 28, December 1
Civilian clothes for soldiers,
    November 9
Clapp, Maj. Dexter E., October
    19
Clark County, Missouri, 4

Clark, Pvt. Abraham J., July 29,
    September 27, October 31,
    November 6; footnote 26
Company G, 21st Missouri, 6, 7, 8,
    July 8–September 15, October
    5, 9, December 7 [also see 21st
    Missouri Infantry]
Confederacy: see South
Confederate sentiment after the
    war, October 17
Confederate soldiers, 4, 5
Conroy, Mr., July 17
Corinth, Battle of, 5
Corinth, Mississippi, 5
Counterfeiting, November 5, 11

Dancing, July 17, 29, August 1,
    4, 30, September 1, 8, 10, 13,
    October 17, December 9, 10
Dauphin Street, Mobile, October
    21
Davis, Pvt. C. C., November 11,
    December 27
Decatur, Illinois, June 29
Denney, Pvt. John H., October 12;
    footnote 67
De Russy, Gen. Gustavus Adolphus,
    December 14, 15, 17; footnote 126
Dessertion, August 9, 18, 24,
    September 5, 6, November 11,
    December 6, 11, 27, 89
Devault, Pvt. Samuel, November
    2, 6, December 5
Diarrhea, September 7, October
    8; footnote 48 [also see Illness]
Disease: see Illness, Drunkenness
Disorder: see Violence, Theft,
    Counterfeiting, Rape
Dr. Harcus Show, November 14
Drew, Frank, November 4;
    footnote 86
Drunkenness, July 25, 30, 31,
    August 6, 7, 12, 16, 28–30,
    September 15, 20, 27, October

4, 6, 9, 12, 15, 16, 18, 22, 30,
November 3, 7, 10, 17, 19, 28,
December 4, 6, 7, 15, 25, 30, 31

11th Wisconsin Volunteer Infantry
Regiment, August 24; *footnote*
40
86th United States Colored Infantry
Regiment, November 7; *footnote*
92

Fariola, Lt. Col. Octave L. F. E.,
July 22, August 6, 31, September
3, 11–14; *footnote* 21
15th United States Infantry
Regiment (Regular Army),
October 15, 22, December 7,
14, 15; *footnote* 69 [*also see*
Mutiny]
58th Illinois Volunteer Infantry
Regiment, November 13;
footnote 99
Figgins, Pvt. Thomas W., October
20
Fletcher, Gov. Thomas Clement,
October 23; *footnote* 81
Fog, December 18, 25
Following the Flag, November 17
Fort Blakely, 7; December 14, 21,
22
Fort Gaines, July 7
Fort Morgan, July 7
Fort Powell, July 7
14th Regiment Infantry, Corps
de Afrique, *footnote* 92
14th Wisconsin Infantry Veteran
Volunteer Regiment, September
30; *footnote* 60

Glessner, Pvt. Jacob, August 3,
November 10, December 11;
footnote 24
Gore, Catherine Grace Frances
(Moody), December 14

Greathouse, Pvt. John, December
7, 14, 27; *footnotes* 120, 127
Grosskopff, Maj. Edward,
December 14; *footnote* 126
Gumbo, August 1

Hammond, Capt. Barnabas B.,
November 9, 11; *footnote* 95
Harper, Pvt. Alfred L., July 20,
22, 25, August 23, September
3, 5, 6; *footnote* 20
Harris, Lt. Robert R., July 20,
August 20, 26, October 8–13,
16, 26, November 3, 8, 11,
December 2, 27
Harrison, Pvt. Theodore,
December 6, 21, 23
Hellena, Arkansas, July 3
Hitchcock's Press, November 24;
footnote 111
Hobson (Hopson), Pvt. Thomas,
November 11
Holcomb, Pvt. William H.,
December 7; *footnote* 120
Holmes (the sutler), October 18
Hood, Gen. John B., 6
Hopson: *see* Hobson
Horn Island, July 12, 30
Horse races, October 27, November
11, 17, 24
Hospital, 7; November 27
Howard, Charley, December 15
Hunting, December 27–29, 31

Ida Handy, July 1
Illness, 6; September 7, 19, October
8–13, 16, 17, 26, November
3, 27, December 2, 6, 17, 20;
footnote 18 [*also see*
Drunkenness, Injuries]
Indians, June 29
Injuries, October 1, 4, November
7, 11, 12, 20, December 4, 7,
14, 15, 20

Irishmen, August 14, November
19, December 3
Iuka, Battle of, 5

Jackson, Andrew, July 6
Jacksonville, Illinois, June 29
James, Cpl. Amos, August 27,
September 15
Jewelry, December 7
Jones, Pvt. Charles, November 19
Jones, Pvt. Edward, December
31
Johnson, President Andrew,
December 8; *footnote* 122
Johnson, Sgt. Jonathan,
December 15; *footnote* 129

Kentucky, 5
Keokuk, Iowa, June 29,
December 8

Laura, July 8
Lawlessness: *see* Violence, Theft,
Counterfeiting, Rape
Lee, Gen. R. E., 7
Lettour, Pvt. Antwine, November
25
Lewis, Pvt. C. B., November 15,
16, December 28
Longcor, Pvt. George N.,
December 7; *footnote* 120
Longcor, Pvt. Isaac, July 20, 25,
August 23, September 3,
October 11, December 4, 6, 28;
footnotes 20, 118
Loona, Sgt., October 22

McGonigle, Maj. Henry,
November 11, December 15;
footnote 97
McMichael, Pvt. Charles, August
25, September 26, October 4;
footnotes 41, 63
Magnolia, September 3, 10

Magnolia Cemetery, *footnote* 53
Masons, October 15
Massey, Cpl. Frank A., July 20,
25, August 23, December 14;
footnote 20
Massey, Pvt. William F., December
4; *footnotes* 118, 127
Masterson, Pvt. John W.,
December 7, 11, 14; *footnotes*
119, 127
Matlick, Sgt. W. H., December
7; *footnote* 121
Matticker, Cpl., December 14
Mauck, Pvt. Mathew, November
1, 2, 10, December 4, 6; *footnotes*
86, 104, 118
Mauck, Pvt. Reuben, November
12, 16
Memphis, Tennessee, July 2
Mississippi, 5
Missouri, 3, 4, 7, 8
Mobile, Ala., 6–7, July 8,
August 27, 28, September 3, 7,
10–12, September 15–December
24, December 27, 28, 30
Mobile Bay, 6
Mobile Theatre, November 23,
December 2; *footnote* 110
Morrey, Lt. Charles C., September
21; *footnote* 56
Morris, Pvt. Joseph, October 16,
26, 30; *footnote* 71
Moulton, C. F., December 3
Mount Vernon Arsenal, Alabama,
December 25–31; *footnote* 132
Murch, Pvt. Chauncey, October
23, November 3, December 7, 20
Mutiny, December 15

Nashville, Battle of, 6
Negroes, 4, 8, July 14, 22, 26,
August 5, 6, 9, 14, 17, 21–24, 30,
September 3, 12, 14, 15, October

1, 11, 17, 20–22, November 7, 11, 20–22, December 7, 12, 20, 25; *footnotes* 108, 109 [*also see* Racism]

New Orleans, Louisiana, July 6, September 12, October 17; *footnotes* 9, 10, 11, 74

New York City, October 17

Newspapers, October 17 [*also see* Southern newspapers]

96th United States Colored Infantry Regiment, July 22, 26, August 5, 17, 23, 24, 30, 31, September 8; *footnote* 21

119th Illinois Volunteer Infantry Regiment, November 16; *footnote* 102

Onelia, July 30, August 17

Pakenham, Gen. Edward, July 6

Parker, Mrs., August 26, September 2

Pascagoula, Mississippi 8; July 8–September 14; *footnote* 15

Photographs, November 30

Pickett, Miss Alice, August 26

Pickett, Miss Maggie, August 26

Pitts, Pvt, Peter, July 16, October 12, 22; *footnotes* 17, 67

Pleasant Hill, Battle of, 5

Politics: *see* Southern politics

Port Hudson, Louisiana, July 5

Prentice, Gen. Benjamin W., 5

Profanity, October 25, December 15

Prostitution, November 7, December 5

Racism, August 14, 17, 21, 28, 30, September 12, 14, 15, October 21, November 11, 20–22, December 12, 20, 25; *footnotes* 108, 109 [*also see* Negroes]

Rape, July 26

Reconstruction, **8, 9, 89**

Red River Expedition, **5**

Redfish, July 15, August 5

Rees, Lt. Richard, November 9; *footnote* 96

Reindeer, September 3

Rice, Dan, November 28; *footnote* 115

Roberts, Maj. Abel C., September 17, October 28, December 7, 14; *footnote* 52

Robertson, Pvt. William E., November 25

Rolla, December 24

Rollande brothers, November 23, December 2

Roseberry, Pvt. James, November 7, December 4; *footnote* 93

Roseberry, Sgt. Matthias, December 21, 22

Roseberry, Pvt. Rees H., December 6, 21–23

Roseberry, Sgt. Thomas H., July 17, 29, September 11, October 10, November 24, December 23; *footnotes* 19, 112

Round Island, July 12

Russell, Sgt., October 22, December 15

St. Francisville, Missouri, **3**

Schram, Lt. Isaac C., September 17, October 27

Scurvy, September 7

Scopenon grapes, August 26

2nd Northeast Missouri Infantry Regiment, **4–5**

Second Regiment Engineers, Corps de Afrique, *footnote* 21

Senator, December 22; *footnote* 131

Seth B Howes' Great European Circus, November 13, 20

77th Ohio Veteran Volunteer

Infantry Regiment, October 15; *footnote* 70
Sexton brothers, Pvts. Fielling and John, November 11
Shafer, Capt. Emanuel B., December 14, 15; *footnote* 128
Sheeks, Sgt. George W., July 28, September 10; *footnote* 24
Sherrick, Cpl. Joseph, July 28, September 3–5, November 2, 6, December 5; *footnote* 24
Shiloh, Battle of, **5**
Ship Island, July 7
Shotish: *see* Dancing
Sinnott, Lt. Martin N., October 2, December 15
Snyder, Pvt. Sanford, September 15, October 12, 28, November 6, 8, December 20; *footnote* 51
South, 3, **4, 6, 8, 9**
Southern white men, **4, 8;** August 7, 14, 22, November 7, 18, 19
Southern newspapers, August 22, October 17
Southern politics, August 7, November 7, December 2–4; footnotes 34, 91, 117
Southern women, July 14, 17, 18, 26, 29, August 4, 13, 22, 26, 29, 31, September 1, 9, 22, October 17, 25, 29, November 7, 11, 12, 14, 15, 22, 26, 30, December 5, 26 [*also see* Prostitution, Rape]
Spanish Fort, **7**
"Speckled Dick", November 7, December 7; *footnote* 93
Speckled trout, July 15, August 5, 31
Spring Hill, Alabama, November 16, December 9, 24
Springer, Pvt. John, September 18; *footnote* 54
Springer, Sarah Carrie, **9;** July

19, August 2, 5, 23, December 1, 5, 24; *footnote* 135
Stingray, July 27, August 24
Stoughton Bottle, August 30, 31, September 1, 11, October 6, 7, November 3
Swimming, July 13, August 10, September 2

Tennessee, **5, 6**
Tennessee River, **5**
Thayer and Noyes' U. S. Circus, November 13; *footnote* 100
Theatre, November 4, 23, 25
Theft, November 1, 13, 16, December 26
Thompson, Capt. Thomas, November 6
Too Old a Bird to be Caught with Chaff, December 24
Tracy, Capt. Alexander F., September 17, 21; *footnote* 56
Tulley, Sgt., October 22, December 15
Tupelo, Battle of, **5**
21st Missouri Veteran Volunteer Infantry Regiment, **5, 6, 7, 8;** August 15, November 25, December 7, 14, 15, 89, *passim* [*also see* Company G]
24th Missouri Infantry Regiment, August 15; *footnote* 38

United Circus, November 13; *footnotes* 100, 101
U. S. Marine Hospital, Mobile, November 27

Vicksburg, Mississippi, July 4
Violence, July 20, 25, 26, August 5, 6, 9, 14, 16, 17, September 4, 11, October 1, 4, 12–16, 20, 23–28, 31, November 1, 7, 10, 12, 18, 19–22, 29, December 4, 7, 14, 15,

31; *footnotes* 108, 109
Virginia, 7
Wagoner, Pvt. George, December 14
Washington County, Ohio, 3
Watertown, Ohio, 3
Welch, Mr., August 1, 4
Whetstone, Sgt. Jasper N., July 28, 29; *footnote* 25
Whiskey: *see* Drunkenness
Whitely, Pvt. Burr H., November 25
Wilsey, November 19, December 28–30
Wilson, Pvt. James K. P., October 20

Wilson, Pvt. John C., November 25
Women: *see* Southern women
Wood, Gen. Thomas John, October 23; *footnote* 82
Wort, Pvt. Barry B., November 25
Wright, Pvt. Joseph S., December 14

Yealey, Pvt. Alfred, August 9, 20; *footnote* 35

Zephyr, September 11; *footnote* 50